Messages
from your
Future self

MARIE CRYSTAL KUENY

First published in 2025 by Onyx Publishing, an imprint of Notebook Group Limited, Arden House, Deepdale Business Park, Bakewell, Derbyshire, DE45 1GT.

www.onyxpublishing.com
ISBN: 9781913206345

Stories and testimonials in this book are based on true events, but names, details, and identifying characteristics have been changed to protect privacy.

A CIP catalogue record for this book is available from the British Library.

Typeset by Onyx Publishing of Notebook Group Limited.

ONYX PUBLISHING

To my Great Grandma Carol who always knew I was born to write.

And to my children, may you always trust your voice and
follow your dreams!

CONTENTS

INTRODUCTION:
WELCOME TO THE DREAMER WITHIN

———

*Trust the whispers of your soul, for within them lies the divine guidance you
seek. Believe in yourself, for you are a sacred vessel of limitless potential.
When you align your spirit with the universe, miracles unfold, and your path
becomes illuminated with boundless possibilities.*

—Your Future Self

DEAR GODDESS,
WHAT IF YOUR PURPOSE here on Earth transcends mere
survival? What if it stretches beyond the daily grind that tears
down your energy and wears away the essence of your spirit? What if (and
take a deep breath as you read this) you are meant to soar and live your
wildest dreams in a state of flow, harmony, and enchantment?

What if you could directly receive messages from your future self? Your
highest self? What if those messages encouraged you to live out your
passions and purpose with complete clarity, confidence, and conviction?

I invite you into this sacred space. I invite you to play in the energy of
possibility.

You feel the longing for something *more* in your soul, don't you? The deep, primal need to curate a life that feels radiant is present with each beat of your heart. It's okay to admit this. During our time together, I will urge you to fully embody these desires. It is safe to do so here. In fact, denying yourself the life you are meant for is an act of self-harm. It is absolutely necessary for us to reclaim your sovereign, divine right to a life of purpose and passion, together.

As an international bestselling author of the empowering book *Powerhouse Women: Survivor to Thriver,* I fully understand the immense challenges that women continue to face in our world. Whether we consider issues pertaining to gender inequality (including a persistent wage gap), the seemingly unicorn aspiration of work–life balance, or underrepresentation in leadership roles (despite the fact that companies with a higher percentage of women on their leadership teams on average have higher financial returns), women have certainly been handed the short end of the stick in many ways. Let's also not forget about the societal pressures and expectations put on women to "be it all and do it all" that can lead to feelings of self-doubt, inadequacy, and stress both at home and in the workplace.

I hear from women around the globe who all say that this universal pattern of doubt, guilt, and uncertainty is keeping them awake at night and restless during the day. It's exhausting. Yet I also know that when these people come together as compassionate powerhouse women, they not only empower and inspire each other, but also shift the lives of future generations for the better. It is with this unwavering belief in the collective power of women that I present you with a way to move forward and prosper. This book will guide you through this process of transformation in the most loving and gentle way. We will explore actionable steps which will bring shifts in your inner and outer world and which you can take starting today. I refer to these steps as "inspired action."

I intimately know the struggle that comes when you feel disconnected from your highest self. I know how it feels to yearn for a life that inspires passion and makes a positive and meaningful difference in the world (and how it feels to be very far from that). It is from this place of understanding that I extend my hand to guide you on your own unique path. When we stay in the present moment and take inspired action instead of ruminating on past harm and pain, we create a life that feels like a magnificent journey.

This book can serve as a bridge between the present moment and the glorious future that awaits you, if you allow it to. As you progress through its pages, you will discover profound messages that your future self, with all her wisdom and love, has sent to guide you. These messages will remind you of your inherent worth, your boundless potential, and the remarkable difference you are destined to make in the world. This is because when we get clear and focused on what we truly desire (rather than what society tells us we should want), the universe delivers what our souls need. With this mission in mind, I invite you to reclaim your inner Goddess in the pages ahead; to rise above the limitations that have held you back; to step boldly into a life that brims with confidence, hope, and unshakeable purpose. This is your time to reconnect with the spark that resides within you. That spark yearns to become a flame; to radiate its brilliance; to illuminate your path. It is time to claim your legacy.

There will be times in these pages where I refer to your dreams and aspirations as your "personal legend." This phrase comes from Paulo Coelho's *The Alchemist*, one of my favorite books of all time. It changed my entire perspective on life when I first read it. In the book, a personal legend is essentially what your soul's purpose on Earth is. It is that longing that you have possibly had since childhood. It is the destiny that you are called to and that will keep calling out to you until you listen and take inspired action.

This journey is not meant to be a solo adventure. For this reason, think of this book as your sanctuary; like a gathering place where likeminded women come together to support and uplift one another. In this sacred space, we honor the power of intuition and community as a guiding compass that helps us to align our dreams with our genuine desire to make a positive impact on the world.

We Are Never Ready. We Are Always Ready.

Once upon a time, I found myself filled with uncertainty and self-doubt. I had accomplished many great things in life—I had bought a house before turning thirty and earned a master's degree—and I carried big dreams about changing the world for the better, but deep inside, I felt trapped in a toxic relationship. I also knew I was still playing small, in pretty much every area of my life. I feared that my life was not going the way I had envisioned it.

Then, a momentous event occurred: I discovered that I was pregnant with my first child. Fear, doubt, and confusion gripped my heart. How could I navigate this new chapter in my life? Questions and fears swirled in my mind. Was I ready to be a mother? Could I still pursue my dreams while facing the challenges that lie ahead?

Amid my inner turmoil, something shifted within me. The life growing inside me became a catalyst for hope and strength. It was as if this precious being was urging me to rise above my fears and to take control of my own destiny. With newfound determination, I made the courageous decision to end the harmful relationship that was holding me back. It may seem counterintuitive to choose to become a single parent right at the beginning of a child's life, but my reconnection to my intuition finally brought me enough clarity for me to know that it was the best decision for us all. As I stepped away from that toxicity, I sought solace and strength in the people who showed true care for me, and as I did so, I began to uncover the power I had always held within. I explored various avenues that I knew could lead me to the life I craved, starting with my entrepreneurial journey. This began with me working for direct sales companies, and it sparked a glimmer of excitement within me. Deep down, though, I knew that, one day, I would need to create something of my own. My life's work could not be to sell other people's dreams. I needed something that felt true to my heart and that would help others exponentially.

After years of navigating various careers and businesses, a "soul calling" whispered to me: a vision of Goddess of Light Retreats. I longed to create a sacred space for women, where they could reconnect to their intuition, heal from the inside out, and feel complete, without judgment.

In truth, the seed of this dream had been planted within me years before, in my early twenties. I had been helping to facilitate women's retreats and meditation retreats at a Zen Buddhist community I belonged to, and this experience had changed my life. I wanted to share that transformative process with more women.

Now that this soul calling felt crystal clear, I set out on a mission to create those Goddess of Light Retreats I had envisioned. Little did I know that this would act as a turning point for so many women who would go on to feel empowered enough to embrace their own passions and purpose. Through these retreats, I aimed to remind my attendants that they are always supported and connected to one another, to Mother Earth, and to their highest wisdom.

With every step I took on this new path, I felt the exhilaration that comes with stepping into one's power. I quickly realized that the challenges I had faced in the past had, in fact, not been obstacles, but opportunities for growth. I poured my heart and soul into building my retreats, and with each one, I witnessed the lifechanging power they had. Soon enough, I was receiving messages from the retreat attendees about their experiences, and this feedback assured me that my career transition to a transformational leader had been divinely inspired. Some said:

- "It was a day filled with peace, kindness, enchantment, and pure bliss."
- "I gained new friends, a sense of peace and love, a reminder to stop and relax and to remember that it's okay to not be okay."
- "I never in my life experienced anything so cool!"
- "I gained confidence and the power to retain my power. The ability to move the light energy in my body. The permission to take care of me."
- "I pushed through fears of being vulnerable with strangers and allowed myself to experience new and raw beauty!"

- "I feel like if I say this was lifechanging, you might think I'm exaggerating. I'm not. I learned so many tools to help me relax, tune into nature, and just slow down."

Today, years later, I stand proud as a mother, dreamer, creator, founder, and I want you to also feel the incredible fulfillment that comes from leading with your soul's passions. I have learned that, even in the face of fear and uncertainty, we have the power to shape our lives and make a difference. My own journey brought me to a path of empowerment, healing, and connection, and now, I continue to inspire women through Goddess of Light Retreats and to support them as they take inspired action to make their personal legends a reality. This has led for women I coach to speak on stages, start their own business, pursue a new relationship, travel to their dream destinations, transform or uplevel their career, increase joy and connection with their children, or simply to be more present in their everyday life and truly embody their highest version of themselves. Throughout all these journeys, I am reminded of the limitless potential that lies within each and every one of us.

When times are challenging, uncertain, and even painful, remember that near every shadow is a light. You can shift your consciousness to a higher state by acknowledging, then releasing, fear of your shadows and focusing on the light within.

In times when this light appears to be dimmed, or you are struggling to connect to it, it is okay to look for the light around you, whether in the beauty of a sunrise or the laugh of a child. Do not fear the dark or push it away though. Even darkness contains wisdom to be gained.

Go into nature, connect with your community, confide in a mentor, and practice the tools I have laid out for you in the following chapters, and you will find the light.

There is always a path back to your higher knowing.

The messages in this book are designed to activate and awaken your higher self. They are keys that can and will unlock doors to what you have been missing in your life up until now; that empty space that has been waiting to be filled by your divine calling. You are never alone, my dear sisters, and your dreams are valid, worthy, and achievable.

What to Expect

In this book, I will be acting as a guide on your journey to self-discovery. As I lead the way, you will learn how to awaken your energetic power (both within yourself and in your environment) and how to raise your frequency, so you can release your bonds to the past, cultivate gratitude for the present, and align with your future self. Do this, and each day will become an opportunity for you to reclaim your highest vision. We will explore how you can show up with confidence and conviction and how you can trust yourself to such an extent that you are unshakeable, even when the tough stuff comes along. By the end of this book, your (metaphorical) roots will be planted so deeply that you will be able to bend and not break when the winds of change and challenge come along. (As we know, change is the only constant in life.) Perhaps most importantly, we will explore how you can become the woman of your dreams; how you can intentionally breathe life into who you desire to be. I will share the methods I have used to tap into my soul's calling, and I will help you to create your own inspired action steps and blueprint, so you can step into a life that you are enchanted by.

While this book is not meant to be used purely as a manifestation guide, you may begin to notice that what you truly desire is being naturally drawn toward you as you move through the process. This may not immediately happen in the external realm, but you will probably feel it from within your heart and soul. That is where it all begins.

I have taught countless women to integrate their highest-self messages into their lives, and I am so looking forward to watching this magic awaken within you, too!

What is "magic", though? Magic is the ability to create change within you and in your environment through inspired action. It is also the practice of harnessing the energy that is within and around you. It is the ability to use your intuition, your pure loving nature, your curiosity, your light, your shadows, all of it, to make tangible shifts in your internal and external world. There are also times in this book I use the term "magic" to encompass that pure feeling of bliss that often washes over us in the most beautiful and surprising ways. Magic (in the way I am using the term) is a reflection of your own inner power.

By taking the inspired action outlined in this book, you will bring forward your power in new ways, beyond what you have previously believed was possible. You will not only be able to clearly visualize your purpose, but you will also have the tools and courage necessary to bring them to life. Throughout, I will help you set your inner fire ablaze, embrace your intuition, and connect with other incredible women in the sacred spaces where magic happens. You will discover the power of your compassion and ambition, transform lives, and create a ripple effect of positive change, all while setting the stage for your own personal legacy.

To set yourself up well for this journey you are about to take, decide in advance to view any setbacks you face as steppingstones to success. View every challenge as an opportunity for growth. Trust the process and have faith in your own abilities. Remember that even the smallest steps forward are significant in that they contribute to your overall progress. If it ever feels like you have taken a step back, that's okay too. Take a deep breath, find the lesson, rest if you need a break, then try again. There is no perfection in progress. There is no progress without failing forward.

To receive the most value from the messages in this book (and to get the fastest results), I recommend reading from beginning to end while taking regular breaks to process the information and to take the recommended inspired action before coming right back for more. You can also flip to the Study Guide/Book Club Guide at the end of this book after you finish each chapter, for maximum benefits.

I have grouped this book into five sections, each with two chapters. The tagline of my business (and the core of what I teach within my Goddess of Light Retreats) is "Heal. Align. Amplify. Flow." This is the sequence I walk my clients through, and the first four sections of this book therefore correspond to this sequence. Each of these sections forms a layer that builds upon the previous one. Progress through each section purposefully and chronologically, and you will ultimately reclaim your sacred wisdom and create a life of purpose and enchantment. The fifth and final section is titled "Create", because by that point, you will have reached a place within where you are ready to stop dreaming about the life you are desiring and to instead step into creating every aspect of it.

To support your path even further, you will find two key distinct inclusions at the conclusion of each chapter. The first is a "Goddess Inspiration" section. The second is the "Inspired Action" section. Let's explore both, so you will know how you can get the most value out of them.

The "Goddess Inspiration" Sections

I love using ancient Goddess mythology for inspiration (as well as the words of powerful women of times past and present) for guidance and encouragement. They serve as role models that encourage us to keep stepping into our highest, most powerful selves.

Research across various fields of personal development has consistently highlighted the profound impact that role models (whether real people or mythical archetypes) have on our personal growth and transformation. Specifically, studies in psychology have shown that exposure to inspiring figures (again, whether real or mythical) can stimulate our imagination, enhance our self-belief, and amplify our motivation to pursue goals. One such study conducted by psychologists at the University of California explored the effects of exposure to inspiring figures on participants' self-efficacy (a key factor in personal development). They found that those who were exposed to stories about and depictions of powerful and accomplished individuals reported higher levels of self-efficacy compared to those in a control group. This suggests that when we draw inspiration from role models (including the Goddesses we will explore throughout this book), we enhance our belief in our own abilities. This can be all the encouragement we need to take inspired action. Additionally, research conducted by social psychologists at the University of Oxford demonstrated that identification with powerful and admired figures can positively influence our sense of identity. So, by engaging with the stories and qualities of Goddesses who epitomize strength, wisdom, and purpose, we can fuel our confidence and self-assurance. Exposure to uplifting and inspiring narratives can have a profound impact on our wellbeing and overall life satisfaction. When we delve into the realms of ancient Goddesses and their empowering stories, we tap into inspiration that transcends time and cultural boundaries. The qualities and strengths attributed to these Goddesses mirror our own innate potential, reminding us of the vast reservoir of power and wisdom that resides within us.

When I was younger, whenever someone asked me who my role model or hero was, I responded, "My mom." While that is still true, we often need to look beyond our childhoods and even the communities in which we were raised when we are striving to create something that no one in our inner circle has before. Becoming the woman of our dreams requires us to expand far beyond our comfort zone and into our genius zone (we will be exploring this in Chapter 8), and this often requires us to take those first leaps before we even know what our genius zone is, or how the transformation will even happen. This is why having models of what is *possible* (not of what has historically been *done before* in our circles) significantly increases the likelihood of us achieving goals that expand far beyond what we once believed to be "realistic." If I had stayed in the arena of what "realistic" looked like in my circles, I never would have facilitated retreats, written this book, or even graduated from university. Thank goodness we can look up to visionaries and changemakers!

When we integrate the wisdom and energy of both ancient Goddesses *and* modern research into our lives, we leverage the power of both ancient traditions and contemporary knowledge, fostering a synergistic approach to personal development. This is a path that merges the timeless wisdom of the divine feminine with the empirical evidence supporting the transformative power of self-work. This is where psychology and spirituality intersect beautifully.

As you read the descriptions of each Goddess in the "Goddess Inspiration" sections, feel into which ones deeply resonate in your core. These Goddesses each inspire and empower, provide guidance and protection, and bring forth qualities of wisdom, strength, creativity, and love in their own way. Learn which energies your future self is wanting to embrace or become reacquainted with so you can carry them with you as you step into the life of your dreams.

Please note that the descriptions in the "Goddess Inspiration" sections are based on popular mythical and cultural representations of each deity and are written for inspirational and symbolic purposes only. Interpretations of these figures may vary across individuals and cultures.

The "Inspired Action" Sections

Years ago, when I was coaching clinicians through taking their business online, I led a weekly call that I titled "Imperfect Action." The goal of these calls was for the practitioners to take specific steps that would produce tangible results and get them closer to their objectives, even if those actions felt imperfect (perfectionism prevents many businesses from achieving radical growth). One day, while I was leading one of these meetings, I had a serious lightbulb moment, and my world shifted. In that moment, I realized that, when we take "imperfect action", we actually run the risk of going down the completely wrong path. We may climb metaphorical mountains and find the courage to swim across seas with crocodiles, only to discover we are still nowhere near where we desire to be. When this happens, we can become disillusioned, and we can wonder if our goals are even achievable, or, worse yet, whether they are worthy of our time, energy, and resources. Why waste years and face countless unnecessary roadblocks when it can be so much more rewarding (and time-effective) to take *inspired action*? Sure, we can learn meaningful lessons when we simply forge ahead with imperfect action, faking it 'til we make it, stomping down the road of imposter syndrome, and dealing with the hustle and grind of just "trying to get ahead", but if we make a switch to inspired action and tune inward, we not only create a shortcut for ourselves (saving years, or maybe even lifetimes, of running full force in the wrong direction), but we can also feel more at peace. We can learn to trust ourselves more deeply and to enjoy the journey. We cannot always predict what the end result of inspired action will be, but we can always trust that we are heading in the right direction.

Inspired action allows us to tap into the wisdom of our divine feminine essence while also embracing our divine masculine energy. It is in the harmonious balance of yin and yang—of inner listening and action—that true transformation awaits. Our feminine essence embodies "inspiration", and our masculine essence embodies "action." Inspired action.

Note that when I refer to "feminine" and "masculine" energy, I am not referring to gender roles. We all have both feminine and masculine energy within us. Inspired action is about harnessing this energy in a holistic way, for the greatest benefit. Divine feminine energy entails being attuned to your inner guidance, or, as the title of this book suggests, listening to messages from your future self or your higher self. This version of you sees the bigger picture of this lifetime (and every lifetime) and the outcomes of the decisions you make. It loves connecting to others and to mother nature, engaging in creative self-expression, setting boundaries, fostering radical self-compassion, and speaking its truth with clarity and confidence. Divine masculine energy, on the other hand, loves taking purposeful action, knowing its self-worth, uplifting others, acting with integrity, not being influenced by societal pressures, and living authentically.

When you combine your feminine energy with your masculine energy, your chances of having a fulfilling life drive up astronomically. Doing so gives you more balance and moves you faster toward your true purpose, while keeping you aligned with your personal values.

Definitions

Before we dive in, I want to speak into the terms "higher power" and "higher self."

It is my personal belief, based on decades spent studying various religions and cultures, that there is a spiritual energy that resides within each of us. This energy, when emitted in various frequencies, creates all that we see, feel, and experience around us. This manifests for everyone in a different way, as we are all on a unique journey. We can all tap into this higher power, or, as some call it, the "universal oneness", which has no limits and exists on, in, around, and beyond what we know with our conscious and unconscious awareness.

If you are more scientifically minded or business oriented, you may prefer to substitute the words "Goddess", "Inner Goddess", and "higher/future self" with "inner coach". The term "inner coach" was coined by Carol Dweck, a renowned psychologist who has helped millions of people understand that their talents, abilities, and even types and levels of intelligence are open to growth, and are not fixed. Please use the terminology that aligns with you most.

Finally, allow me to expand on what I mean when I refer to "dreams" and "desires."

When I speak about dreams and desires, I am always referring to desires that contribute to your personal greater good and the collective greater good. Any desires that are based on the ego only, or that have the potential to harm you or others, are not messages from your higher or future self. If you have any such thoughts, feelings, or impulses, please seek professional assistance immediately. I trust that if you are reading this book, your intentions are pure and that you truly want to co-create a world that is more joyful, peaceful, and loving for all. Any thoughts, feelings, and actions that are harmful to others always come from a place of fear and "lack", which is what we are looking to release in this book. In this space, we welcome in strength, vitality, connection, beauty, kindness, compassion, empathy, understanding, generosity, harmony, gratitude, resilience, authenticity, collaboration, forgiveness, acceptance, unity, wisdom, and love.

The time is now. Let us begin.

Goddess Inspiration: Athena (Empowered Wisdom)

Athena, the Greek Goddess of wisdom, strategy, and intellectual prowess, stands as a beacon of inspiration for those seeking empowerment and fulfillment. According to ancient Greek mythology, she helped many heroes during their adventures, including Odysseus, Hercules, and Perseus, and her wisdom was sought after by those seeking brilliance and courage.

Athena was known for her strategic planning. She would always consider the bigger picture and devise effective approaches to overcome challenges. Therefore, embodying Athena's strategic mindset means assessing situations, setting clear objectives, and developing well-thought-out plans to achieve success. It involves considering various options, anticipating potential obstacles, and adapting strategies as needed.

Athena also encourages us to seek collaboration and counsel. While she embodies wisdom and strategic thinking as an individual, she also recognizes the value of collective intelligence. Therefore, seeking out a mentor, guide, or coach is a powerful choice that embodies Athena's essence of wisdom and strategy. A mentor, guide, or coach can provide valuable insights and perspectives based on their experiences and expertise. (I hope that this book serves as a sort of mentor to you!)

When I was first contemplating changing careers from a school counselor to an independent consultant to start my own business, I knew that I couldn't do it alone, but going back to traditional school also didn't feel like the right fit for me. I already had a master's degree, and with a third child on the way, I needed to create a business that was designed around my life. Adjusting my life to fit a more traditional model wasn't going to work for me.

I remembered Athena's teachings about empowered wisdom and decided to sign up for some free webinars and to schedule clarity calls with several business coaches. Before long, I found one that I aligned with. But I didn't stop there. I created a team of support around me that could help me fill the gaps in my knowledge, skills, and confidence. By allowing the energy of Athena's wisdom to come through, I learned to lean into the teachings of my coaches to get the results I desired.

Remember that seeking support from a mentor, guide, or coach will serve you best when you do so through a reciprocal relationship. Such a dynamic is not just about receiving advice; it is also about actively engaging with your mentor, asking questions, and seeking their input. Be open to constructive feedback and be willing to reflect on and integrate their guidance into your own decision-making processes.

The Goddess Athena is someone whose energy you want with you as you start any new venture, partnership, or life transition.

Inspired Action

If you are to receive your future self's messages and then take the steps needed toward your desires, you need a solid foundation of self-trust and confidence. As a gift to you, I have created a virtual mini-retreat, The Goddess Activation Hour, to help you tune into your inner Goddess's wisdom and to concurrently elevate your self-belief and confidence. Download it now to activate your Goddess energy at www.goddessoflightretreats.com/goddessgift. Please do this before moving on.

1

Heal

1

BEGIN WITH RADICAL SELF-COMPASSION

Surrender to what is. Let go of what was. Have faith in what will be.
—Sonia Ricotti

HISTORICALLY, WOMEN HAVE BEEN TAUGHT TO buy the into "good girl" syndrome, which ultimately means doing it all for everyone else and neglecting their own needs, values, and desires. Releasing this "good girl" identity and embracing your "powerful co-creator" identity will be your first step to self-actualization, or in other words, your full potential. You may be good at setting these boundaries already, but most women I meet could use a little support here. If you identify as a "people-pleaser", "empath", or "perfectionist", this is a good sign that too much of your energy is going outward.

This may feel strange to accept, but you should never—and I mean never—make major life decisions based on someone else's desires for you. Your mother wants you to stay in your hometown so you can have Sunday meals together, but your heart is longing to move to Paris for a year and accept an amazing temp job offer there? Go! Find alternative ways to show her that you love her and enjoy this once-in-a-lifetime experience. Your husband is begging you to have one more child, but you already feel constrained with two, and the thought of another feels terrifying? Don't do it—at least, not until you feel confident that it is the best choice for you. Your employee wants to be promoted, but you aren't sure you can trust them with more responsibility because they have yet to show that their skills are a match for your business? Or (on the flipside) an employer wants you to add duties to your already extensive load of responsibilities and is unwilling to fairly compensate you? Wait and have a conversation to bring more clarity into this important work relationship. Just because someone else wants or even "needs", something of you, does not mean you have to say yes.

During my first several years as a school counselor, I read *The Giving Tree* by Shel Silverstein to my students. My intention was to help them understand empathy and generosity. I thought the message the book offered was a positive one. As my life became more demanding and complex and more people started vying for my time and attention, however, my interpretation of this book, which I had initially viewed as a beautiful story of compassion, changed for me. In fact, I became appalled while reading it. *No, tree! Stop letting the boy take everything you have! That is not friendship, it is manipulation!* I mean, seriously, when would someone who gave a damn about the tree come along? Everything was taken from it until it was a mere stump. From that point onward, I stopped reading this book to my students and made sure that it was not in my own children's personal library.

If I just tainted your love for this classic, sorry, not sorry. It is time for us to stop giving and giving until we have nothing left, especially to those who do not completely appreciate what we offer. Generosity and kindness are core values of mine, and I love giving when and what I can, but I have also learned that I need to have boundaries around my generosity if I am to remain healthy in the process.

For a while, I was angry with myself for letting others make decisions for me and take advantage of my kindness. I had allowed family and friends to influence huge decisions I had made, from where I lived and the career I sought to the way I dressed (to a degree). Perhaps unsurprisingly, I ultimately reached a dark place. I felt like I didn't know who I was. I had so desperately wanted to be liked that I had been afraid of letting anyone see the "real me", and so I had allowed myself to listen to everyone else's opinions instead of my own inner wisdom. Truth be told, I completely forgot I even had this sacred wisdom. People-pleasing felt safe, and so I hid behind it. For a while, this worked. Until it didn't.

When we are consumed by other people's stories, worries, requests, and demands, there is no space for presence with oneself. This is a dangerous place to be. I once read that some people would rather do anything than spend fifteen minutes alone with themselves with no agenda or distraction, and I think that perfectly demonstrates what we are talking about here.

How can you possibly have joy in your life and receive the wisdom of your highest self if you are so disconnected from the most important relationship you will ever have: the one with yourself? It is time we change this pattern. Even if you feel that you have a strong relationship with the Divine, the Creator, Universal Mother, God, or the Great Spirit, I ask you again, what is the relationship you have with *you*? I have met plenty of people who say that they talk to their friends and family every day, but ask them to be present with themselves for a few minutes of inner reflection, and they will stare at you like you just asked them to commit a heinous crime.

I believe what blocks us from having an amazingly joyful and blessed connection with ourselves is shame, self-blame, and self-criticism. These are rooted in others people's stories about the world and themselves that they had projected onto us when we were young (and were taken in by us as truth). They are also rooted in the people-pleasing tendencies that are all-too-often passed down to women in harmful generational cycles. Furthermore, it is normalized for people to belittle, make fun of, and downright speak harmfully about themselves and others, and this pattern is quickly picked up on by our younger selves and transmuted into negative self-talk. This places a massive barrier between our present self and the self we are wanting to become.

The good news is, there is an antidote to shame, self-blame, and self-criticism (and therefore all the people-pleasing and self-negating you may have been doing): self-compassion. I like to use the phrase "radical self-compassion", because the idea of having limitless self-compassion is quite radical (the definition of "radical" being "far-reaching or extreme"). One of the world's leading self-compassion researchers, Dr. Kristin Neff (essentially the mother of self-compassion research), defines radical self-compassion as "treating ourselves with the same kindness, care, and understanding that we would offer to a good friend." It is an active practice that involves acknowledging your struggles and imperfections with love and acceptance. It allows you to navigate the challenges of life with grace, resilience, and a deep sense of inner peace and fulfillment. It is when we deeply love ourselves that we can hear, with crystal clarity, the next steps we are meant to take on our journey.

Imagine a life where you approach your goals and aspirations with a deep sense of self-love and acceptance. Instead of shaming yourself for every misstep, you respond with tenderness and understanding. You acknowledge the fact that growth and progress are not linear, but a winding journey of ups and downs. Each stumble becomes an opportunity for learning and growth rather than a reason to give up. Such a life is a possible for you.

This is not to say you should excuse yourself of any sense of self-responsibility for your actions. If you break something, you fix it. If you say something you wish you could take back, you apologize and make a concerted effort to never speak that way again. If you make a mistake, you make amends as thoroughly as you can. Then, you move on. What radical self-compassion proposes is not denial of personal responsibility, but a state of being where you do not dwell on that misspoken word for days on end; where maybe you hold a release ceremony for the harm you unintentionally caused; where regret no longer keeps you awake at night, because you have learned how to offer yourself grace. With radical self-compassion, space and energy is freed and cleared in your mind, body, and energy field, and there is greater opportunity for you to move forward in pursuing your purpose and co-creating the life you truly desire. Dr. Neff states, "Individuals who are more self-compassionate tend to have greater happiness, life satisfaction, and motivation, [along with] better relationships and physical health, and less anxiety and depression." Couldn't we all use some of that in our lives?

Cultivating self-compassion is one of the first steps to ensuring you are ready to receive those messages from your higher self. Your higher self wants nothing more than for you to feel so complete and joyful in who you are, as you are.

If you are not there yet, that is okay! Have compassion for the fact that you not yet being fully self-compassionate.

(Read that one more time.)

You have the right to self-compassion, and moment by moment, the more you practice it, you will eventually feel that a giant weight has been lifted, and you will breathe easier. From that moment (and with continued practice), you will know then that you have shifted into a state of radical self-compassion.

Exercising Radical Self-Compassion

"Marie, that sounds nice, but how can I be more self-compassionate when my first instinct is to respond with criticism or doubt when I make a mistake?" I am glad you asked! Here are a few ways in which you can take self-compassion to the next level, so that you are more deeply attuned to your sacred wisdom.

Acknowledge Imperfections
Understand that nobody is perfect and it is okay to make mistakes or have flaws. Instead of being overly critical of yourself for any missteps, treat yourself with kindness and remind yourself that these imperfections are part of being human.

I know this can be easier said than done. My sun sign is in Virgo, so perfectionism is my right-hand frenemy. Still, by embracing the fact that every human on this planet is interesting and unique *because* of (not despite of) their imperfections, you can ease the burden to be Insta-worthy every moment.

Set Realistic Expectations

Driven individuals often set very high expectations for themselves, and this can lead to burnout and disappointment. Practice self-compassion by reminding yourself that it is okay to not achieve everything all at once. Break your goals into manageable steps and celebrate your progress along the way. (Later in this book, I will guide you through a process that has helped me to manage the audacious goals I have for myself.)

You can have your cake and eat it all, but your digestive system will be much better off if you don't eat it all in one sitting (and maybe share a few slices, too)!

Practice Self-Care

Prioritize self-care as a non-negotiable part of your routine. This includes getting enough sleep (seven hours, minimum), eating nourishing foods, exercising regularly (walking, dancing, and yoga all count!), and finding time for relaxation and activities you enjoy (leisure time is so important that it is listed as an essential component for high achievers in *The 5 AM Club* by Robin Sharma). Self-compassion means treating your wellbeing as a priority, not as a luxury.

A couple of years ago, Neferteri Plessy, founder of Single Moms Planet, and my media strategist, encouraged me to define what felt luxurious to me, and to routinely engage in it. For me, it was regular massages. Since then, I have had massages monthly, and it is one of the best things I have ever done for myself. My goal is to eventually increase this to weekly sessions, for maximum benefits.

Think you cannot afford such a luxury? I have learned the hard way that we cannot afford to *not* make self-care an absolute priority. Choose your hard.

Manage Inner Criticism

I spent years teaching youth about the "inner coach" and "inner critic". This concept applies to adults as well. Challenge and reframe your inner critic. When negative thoughts arise, counter them with self-compassionate statements. For example, if you make a mistake, instead of saying, "I always mess up," try, "I made a mistake, but everyone does. I can learn from this." We win or we learn, so at the end of the day, we never lose.

Seek Support

Please do not be afraid to seek support from friends or family, or to join a women's circle. This doesn't have to be therapy (though it could be). Having a support system is certainly therapeutic in itself.

In our society, we often assume that we are stronger (or somehow better) if we handle challenges alone. I am so glad that this "pull yourself up by the bootstraps" mentality is slowly giving way to a more collaborative approach. We are stronger when we open up and are vulnerable with one another; when we share, hold space, and allow ourselves to be supported in both the light times and the dark times.

An important note: we all know that friends and family often want the best for us, but when we change direction or follow our heart's calling, they may be unsure of how to support us, or even acknowledge this new version of ourselves. They may even express concern, because they do not understand why we want to make changes to elevate our life. This is why it can also be essential to have support beyond the four walls of your home, or even beyond the limits of your town.

Set Boundaries

Women often struggle with saying no and setting boundaries. Numerous very highly successful entrepreneurs and businesswomen have told me they would not be where they are now had they not made an ironclad promise to themselves that they would reserve their time for only their highest priorities. By recognizing that it is okay to decline requests or commitments that overwhelm you (or that simply do not align with your highest self), you are embracing the art of self-compassion and clearly telling the universe what you need and do not need at that moment. This may feel incredibly uncomfortable at first. Sit with it and take a deep breath. It will get easier.

Forgive Yourself

Guilt and regret can become an impenetrable barrier between the life you have and the life you truly desire. It can even manifest into physical disease. Thankfully, you have the power to release regret and to offer yourself unconditional forgiveness. Recognize that everyone makes mistakes and that these experiences can serve as valuable lessons and motivation for helping others along the way.

As you pursue your life's purpose, it is all too easy to get caught up in self-doubt, self-criticism, and the never-ending pursuit of perfection. This is where radical self-compassion becomes your most potent tool. By offering yourself kindness, understanding, and forgiveness, you break free from the shackles of self-judgment and find the courage to take risks, learn from failures, and persist in the face of adversity.

Radical self-compassion is not an indulgence. It is a necessary practice if you are to co-create the life you desire. It is the key that unlocks your inner power and places you on the path of personal growth and achievement. When you practice daily self-compassion, you elevate yourself to new heights, you become the woman you need to be, and you become unstoppable in your pursuit of greatness, because you know that your worth is not contingent upon external achievements or validation. You embrace your intrinsic value and allow it to guide your decisions, actions, and relationships.

Wabi Sabi and Liquid Gold

The philosophy of Wabi Sabi originates from Japanese aesthetics, and is rooted in the belief that imperfection, transience, and authenticity hold a unique and captivating beauty. This is personified through the image of a broken teacup: if the cup is pieced together again with gold (rather than discarded), the value of the teacup (though it is now "imperfect") increases, and the item becomes more revered than a "normal" teacup. The teacup is precious not because of what has *not* happened to it, but because of the transformation it has experienced because of what *has* happened to it. Wabi Sabi invites us to see the world through a lens that appreciates the beauty of imperfection and that finds solace in the ever-changing nature of life.

I initially discovered this philosophy when I picked up Arielle Ford's *Wabi Sabi Love* shortly after it was released. Her teachings resonated deeply. I knew that I had fractures within, and was looking for the liquid gold that would mend the cracks. I immediately joined Arielle's coaching program so I could learn how to bring more of this type of love to myself and my relationships.

When my former partner and I purchased our home, I was pregnant with our second child, with no plans of having a third. A small ranch with three bedrooms and a basement therefore seemed perfectly adequate for our little family. Then came a third child, and what once felt like a perfect space for us began to feel cramped at times.

The expected, default attitude toward this might have been frustration. "We need a bigger house. It is not fair that other people can afford mansions and have more money than they know what to do with. I am tired of being in this little house!" However, if I had that kind of approach every day, I would likely make myself very challenging to be around, and the emotional and physical taxation it would create for me would probably cause me to spiral. Even though we all may want to go there at times, this type of energy is not going to manifest anything for me other than feelings of discontentment, and possibly even unworthiness.

Let's being some Wabi Sabi into the mix now. Same situation, different approach: "I know that we will need to move into a larger house within the next few years, but for now, I am so grateful that we have enough room for the five of us and our own backyard to play in. Sometimes it feels a little cramped, but while these children are young, it is nice to be together in a home where everyone feels close and taken care of. I feel so fortunate."

This way of seeing life is not limited to romantic relationships. It is a philosophy for the way we can live each day and each moment. It teaches us to stop judging ourselves, others, and our environments. When we apply the principles of Wabi Sabi to the concept of radical self-compassion, we shift our perspective to create space for self-acceptance, growth, and creativity. After all, Wabi Sabi teaches us to find beauty in the imperfect and to recognize that imperfections are not flaws to be hidden, but distinctive characteristics that make something truly unique and authentic. Wabi Sabi says we should value the process, appreciate our efforts, and find beauty in the imperfect outcomes that come from us taking inspired action and deeply loving ourselves without judgment. It also promotes a kind of inner contentment. If we are always striving for something different from a place of dissatisfaction, disconnection, or "lack", we can reach a place of exhaustion and even develop physical illness. This does not mean that we should not have goals and aspirations that we reach for (far from it), but it does mean that the climb to our goals must be balanced with awareness of the beauty that lies in the present moment.

Wabi Sabi also reminds us that nothing lasts forever. It therefore encourages us to cherish the present moment. This way of being teaches us to let go of the fear of making mistakes or waiting for the perfect opportunity. It reminds us that life and its circumstances are ever-changing, and that it is in those moments of impermanence that growth and transformation can happen.

Authenticity lies at the heart of Wabi Sabi. By embracing our genuine selves, we connect more deeply with others, inspire trust, and create genuine connections that support and nurture our dreams. When we live a Wabi Sabi kind of life, we honor the uniqueness of our journey and open ourselves up to the serendipitous discoveries, unexpected joys, and transformative growth that can only come from embracing imperfection in all its forms.

Let us look at another concrete example of Wabi Sabi living:

When my partner and I purchased our home, I was pregnant with our second child, with no plans of having a third. A small ranch with three bedrooms and a basement therefore seemed perfectly adequate for our little family. Now, however, we have three growing children. So, what once felt like a perfect space for us can feel cramped at times. What's more, my boys' energies and personalities clash too often for them to share a room—they each require their own space, for the sake of everyone in the home!—so this leaves even less space for me and my partner.

The expected, default attitude toward this might be frustration. "We need a bigger house. It is not fair that other people can afford mansions and have more money than they know what to do with. I am tired of being in this little house, with these wild kids!" However, if I had that kind of approach every day, I would likely make myself very challenging to be around, and the emotional and physical taxation it would create for me would probably cause me to spiral. Even though we all may want to go there at times (and that is okay—remember radical self-compassion!), this type of energy is not going to manifest anything for me other than feelings of discontentment, and possibly even unworthiness.

Let's bring some Wabi Sabi into the mix now. Same situation, different approach: "I know that we will need to move into a larger house within the next few years, but for now, I am so grateful that we have enough room for the five of us and our own backyard to play in. Sometimes it feels a little cramped, but while these children are young, it is nice to be together in a home where everyone feels close and taken care of. We are so fortunate."

Notice how the Wabi Sabi approach is filled with very different energy. It has a foundation of gratitude, love, and acceptance, and it does not involve being dishonest or sugarcoating the situation.

Imagine if I were to say each statement around my children. How do you think they would react to each one? With the first, they would be more likely to either model or internalize my complaints and blame. If I adopted the second approach, they would similarly model or internalize an energy of abundance.

Where in your life could you use a little more Wabi Sabi? In the way you treat yourself, maybe? In your relationship? In your friendships? At home or at work? Find where things feel a bit fragmented and fill it in with those liquid gold thoughts and frequencies!

Ancestral Healing

There is one more area which I must draw attention to as we discuss healing and self-compassion: the profound impact of generational trauma and the transformative power of ancestral healing. Often, the pain we carry is not solely our own—it is an unwanted inheritance passed down through generations. Wounds left unresolved in our family lines can imprint patterns of fear, shame, and disconnection on our lives, and on future generations as well. Acknowledging this truth can be both liberating and daunting. Yet, it also offers a profound opportunity to rewrite not only our own stories but also the legacies we leave behind.

Self-compassion is essential in this process. When we confront generational trauma, we may feel anger, sadness, or even guilt for the experiences of our ancestors. These emotions are valid, but they are not the full story. Through self-compassion, we can hold space for these feelings without judgment, recognizing that we are both the keepers and the healers of this inherited pain. We honor our ancestors by acknowledging their struggles while refusing to let their unresolved wounds define our future.

I had the honor of hosting an ancestral healing retreat, Release to Rebirth, with Family Constellations expert Mallory Mammes McClelland. Family Constellations is a therapeutic approach that seeks to uncover and resolve deeply rooted issues within a family system. Developed by Bert Hellinger, this method is based on the idea that unresolved trauma, emotional pain, or imbalances in past generations can affect the well-being and behavior of individuals in the present. By addressing these hidden dynamics, Family Constellations helps to restore harmony and balance within the family system and within the individual. During this retreat, each participant served as representatives of each other's family lineage, to tap into the energy needed to release the burdens that they were never meant to carry generation after generation. It was a beautiful experience that left most of the women feeling freer than ever before. They energetically and intellectually were able to untangle old stories and make a new path for themselves.

According to Mallory, "unprocessed transgenerational trauma is one of the silent barriers to reaching your full potential. It can manifest as blocks in areas such as money, health, career, relationships, and more. On a conscious level, we often believe these blocks are somehow our fault. However, when viewed through the lens of Family Constellations, the true energetic roots of these 'blocks' become clear. Family Constellations allow us to acknowledge the trauma our ancestors experienced and release ourselves from the burden of repeating those patterns. This powerful approach can help you find freedom and create the life you've been dreaming of."

When exploring ancestral healing it becomes clear that forgiveness—both of our ancestors and of ourselves—can be a powerful act of liberation. By choosing to view our heritage through a lens of love and understanding, we can begin to transform the shadows of our lineage into sources of strength and resilience. When I first began to imagine my ancestors behind me as support, I initially saw nothing, and felt alone. However, after just a few hours of working through generational healing, I could see hundreds of ancestors across generations, lifting me up and reminding me that I am infinitely supported and that there is a great field of collective strength behind me – behind us all!

In this work, the threads of self-compassion and ancestral healing are beautifully intertwined. As we show ourselves kindness and patience, we create a safe space to process what may have been suppressed for generations. When we nurture ourselves, we also pave the way for our descendants to inherit healing rather than pain. In this sense, ancestral healing is not just about mending the past—it is an act of hope for the future.

By engaging in this sacred work, we step into a role of empowerment. We honor the sacrifices of our ancestors while consciously choosing to break cycles that no longer serve us. This is the ultimate act of self-compassion: not only healing for ourselves but becoming a beacon of light for those who came before and those who will follow. Through this process, we embody the truth that healing is possible, and through healing, we transform the narrative of our lives and our lineage.

Goddess Inspiration: Kuan Yin (Compassion and Forgiveness)

Kuan Yin (which, in some cultures, is spelled "Guanyin" or "Quan Yin") is a Buddhist Goddess who embodies the power of compassion and loving kindness. She has been my personal guide since I first consciously learned of her in my early twenties while I was practicing at the Original Root Zen Center (though I think her essence and presence were lying dormant in me long before). Kuan Yin embodies unconditional love, and she offers comfort, healing, and guidance to those in need. Just as she extends her loving compassion to all beings, Kuan Yin invites you to cultivate self-compassion and extend that same kindness to others. She teaches us that compassion begins with self-love and acceptance, acknowledgment of our struggles, treating ourselves with kindness and understanding, embracing imperfections, forgiving mistakes, and nurturing our wellbeing. From this place of self-compassion, we can radiate love and empathy to others.

There is a Hawai'ian prayer of reconciliation and forgiveness that has gained more recognition recently, and I feel fits very well here. It is called *Ho'oponopono*. (If you find yourself rereading that and trying (and failing) to say it, you are not the only one, I promise! It is broken down as "Ho-o-pono-pono".) The prayer is simple, yet the energy it emits is so powerful that it opens the portal for compassion to flow through without limitations. There are four parts to this prayer, ideally to be recited one hundred and eight times. If you lose track, I won't tell. Just keep going until it feels complete to you, even if it's only a single repetition. The prayer goes as follows:

> *I am sorry.*
> *Please forgive me.*
> *Thank you.*
> *I love you.*

During one of my biggest meltdowns after my thirty-seven-year-old brother Craig's unexpected passing, I used this prayer to make peace with him and myself. There were so many questions left unanswered; so many words I wished I had (or hadn't) said; so many "what-ifs". I could not shake the uneasiness I felt. Until, that is, I went deep into this prayer. While my children were at their grandfather's house and all was quiet, I allowed my tears to freely flow, and I cried out, "I'm sorry! I'm sorry!"

My feelings crashed over me in full force. *I did everything I could to help him, even when I was still a child myself, but it never felt like enough.* Even though these feelings were tough, "I'm sorry!" helped me to release some of the burdens that I was still carrying. It also allowed me to express "I'm sorry" for the fact that he would never physically witness his daughter growing up, or for the fact that I had not barged my way into his one-bedroom apartment, opened the curtains, and pulled him out of his reclining chair for one more hug before he was gone. Everything that is weighing on the conscious (as well as the unconscious) mind is released through the repetition of these words: "I'm sorry."

Next, "Please forgive me." Even if you think there is nothing to be forgiven, this can also serve as a statement of self-forgiveness. We spend too much of our lives blaming, shaming, and criticizing ourselves for every little thing that doesn't go "right", but what if there is no "right"? What if the only events that happen in life are meant to be (because if they aren't meant to be, they couldn't manifest into reality, could they?). This proclamation of forgiveness can shift your energy into a state of deep compassion for yourself and for others.

The third statement of *Ho'oponopono* is, "Thank you." How beautiful! Thank you, *mahalo, gracias, arigatou, merci, grazie, danke, asante, toda, tack*. In every language, there is an energy of appreciation and lightness to this word. During one of my moments of grief, I deeply and completely thanked my brother for the time he spent with me; for being my best friend and confidant in childhood (even though he was terrible at keeping secrets!); for being the one person who I could be my silliest self around. From the times we made up our own parody songs (similar to "Weird Al" Yankovich) to the times we talked about our nineties nostalgia, I thanked him for every moment he spent with me. Gratitude is the foundation for compassion.

The final piece of the prayer is, "I love you." I love saying, "I love you, I love you, I love you. I love you for your quietness and your wildness. I love you for your crazy days and your calm ways. I love you for the moments shared and for the space you give me. I love you for being you and accepting me for me. I love you completely, unconditionally, wholly, and infinitely. Love is love is love is love." I can direct this inward (to myself) or outward (to someone else).

I invite you to try the *Ho'oponopono* prayer right now. Take a deep breath in, and then do a long exhale out. Repeat, "I am sorry. Please forgive me. Thank you. I love you." This does not need to be directed toward anyone else. This is for you, to expand your connection with your highest self, your past, your future, and every part of you in between and beyond. When we practice loving kindness in our thoughts, words, and actions, we cultivate a sense of gratitude for the interconnectedness of all beings, and we recognize that our actions ripple out and impact the universal oneness.

Inspired Action

Now, it is your turn to practice radical self-compassion. Choose one of the recommendations in this chapter and incorporate it into your daily routine. Set a time on your calendar when you will bring your attention to self-compassion. One of the most powerful and direct ways of practicing radical self-compassion is, simply, saying the *Ho'oponopono* prayer, with your focus tuned inward.

If you would like a complementary printable while you take inspired action, please visit www.goddessoflightretreats.com/hp.

2

RADIANT HEALING

———

The more we attune to peace, the more radiant our lives become.
—Zen Proverb

R ADICAL SELF-COMPASSION AND ACCEPTANCE (WHICH WE laid the foundations for in the previous chapter) is the first step to being able to receive messages from your future self. The second step is to create an energetic blank canvas (or as close to one as you can get) to create the space for your next chapter to unfold. This involves a touch of energy work and a sprinkle of manifestation.

Imagine that every word that has ever been said to you, every perceived harm that has come your way, every story and memory, is a different color of paint that has been splattered across your energetic canvas. The white space disappears quicker and quicker the deeper you dig, doesn't it? To awaken your energetic power, you first must let go of the limiting beliefs, emotional blockages, and unconscious patterns that are keeping you stuck and playing small. This sounds like a big ask, but once you have finished this book and done the work, you will not only have a clear direction on how to achieve this, but you will know that it can be done *with joy and ease.*

In this chapter, I will be sharing insights that may be new to you. If you are like me and you love the intersection of science and soul, it will be one to remember.

Energy Work

In my undergraduate years at the University of Wisconsin–Milwaukee, I was given the opportunity to enter a transformative journey that introduced me to the world of energy healing. I became certified in healing touch and reiki, and in the process, I opened my eyes and heart to profound concepts. I learned about chakras, the subtle body, auras, and quantum energy. Little did I know that this path would lead me to a realm where the senses extended beyond the physical; where the body's energy becomes palpable; where I could witness the interconnectedness of mind, body, and spirit. As I delved deeper into these practices, I marveled at the intricacy of the energetic body and its ability to convey messages and sensations beyond our ordinary perception. Through intentional focus, I discovered that the energy of the body possesses a wealth of information about the person's being that goes far beyond the surface. Soon enough, I could now pick up on the energetic imprints of an individual's history, their emotional landscape, and even at times the physical manifestations within their body. It was as if a new dimension had unfolded before me.

One particular experience from this time stands out vividly in my memory. During a practice session with a fellow student, a strange sensation washed over me the moment I placed my hands near her knee. It felt as though there was a foreign object there; an energy that did not belong. Keep in mind that her legs were fully covered by leggings. Intrigued, I shared my observation with her, half-expecting it to be a mere coincidence. To my astonishment, she confirmed my intuitive perception: she had a metal screw in her knee. In that moment, I realized the incredible depth and accuracy the energetic senses have.

This experience, along with countless others, fueled my thirst for knowledge and intensified my commitment to the study of energy and its profound impact on our wellbeing. I became passionate about exploring the energetic flow within people's bodies, and I grew more and more skilled at identifying areas of stagnation or congestion. I witnessed the transformative power of energy work (and the liberation that comes with it) as I guided the restoration of balance within many individuals.

Understanding and working with the chakras in particular is a powerful tool for self-discovery, healing, and spiritual growth. By identifying the body parts, colors, and challenges associated with each chakra, we can begin to address the root causes of our limitations. Chakra clearing and alignment practices create space for stability, creativity, personal power, love, authentic expression, intuition, and spiritual connection. Modalities such as yoga, qi gong, healing touch and reiki use a deep understanding of the chakra system to elevate the health and wellbeing of the receiver.

Research supporting the effectiveness of energy work has emerged in recent years, providing hope and validation for those seeking to explore these modalities. Such studies have shown promising outcomes in areas such as pain management, stress reduction, enhanced wellbeing, improved mental health, and a holistic approach to care. For instance, it has been demonstrated that energy healing interventions such as reiki and healing touch can reduce pain intensity, alleviate stress and anxiety, improve relaxation, and enhance overall quality of life. These findings highlight the potential of energy work to support our personal journeys of self-discovery, healing, and empowerment.

If you want to find the secrets of the universe, think in terms of energy,
frequency and vibration.
—Nikola Tesla

Many of the women I have met on this path who are drawn to helping others, learning healing tools, and creating more peace and fulfillment in the world have personally experienced the shadow side of life. They have been to hell and back, whether through traumatic childhood experiences, toxic relationships, devasting loss, or complex health struggles. Most have gone through a series of highs and lows that have felt out of their control. Can you relate to this? If so, you will know firsthand how detrimental emotional blockages can be. Energy work is a salve and a preventative measure for these experiences.

Rumi, the renowned poet and mystic, declared, "The wound is the place where the light enters." This also echoes the sentiment behind Wabi Sabi. Energy work provides an opportunity for you to embrace your wounds, shadows, and vulnerabilities as gateways to personal growth and transformation. It is through the exploration of your energetic being that you can unleash your inner power and find balance, healing, and renewed vitality. No longer must you cower from your shadows in fear or shame. Instead, you can shed light on them with love and compassion, embracing them as part of your journey and offering yourself the gift of wholeness.

When I reflect on my own journey, it is evident to me that my body is not just a physical vessel, but a storehouse of energy and a repository of experience, emotion, and memory. Every meaningful thought, emotion, and interaction I have had has imprinted itself upon my energetic being, shaping my perception of the world and influencing my overall health and wellbeing.

My exploration of the energy body has been nothing short of awe inspiring. It has awakened within me a deep reverence for the interconnectedness of all things and a commitment to helping facilitate healing and transformation in others. Today, as an advocate for holistic wellbeing, I find myself utilizing the wisdom and practices of energy work in a variety of transformative ways daily. I have expanded my horizons beyond individual sessions and now also create sanctuaries of healing and renewal. Whether I am working in a home, a workshop space, or a retreat center, I understand the importance of harmonizing my energetic environment to facilitate profound transformations.

Energy Work as a Conductor for Manifestation

The only way we can change our lives is to change our energy.
—Joe Dispenza

This quote by Joe Dispenza perfectly resonates with how I view the power of energy clearing, co-creation, and manifestation. Emotions are energy in motion and energy clearing practices pave the way for the alignment of our thoughts, emotions, and beliefs with our desires. When we make a conscious decision to change, embrace our highest potential, and co-create our reality, the transformation begins instantaneously. This is a powerful reminder that by harnessing the power of our energy, we can create profound shifts in our lives and manifest our dreams.

It is important to note that energy healing practices are even more powerful and swift when combined with inspired action and a deep, unshakeable belief that the universe is co-creating with you to form the life you envision. This sets the stage for manifestation by creating an optimal energetic environment. You become more attuned to your desires, and the universe responds to your elevated energy with synchronicities, opportunities, and guidance. When you couple energy embodiment with inspired action, you move toward your desires as they simultaneously move closer to you in a beautiful dance.

There is a profound truth of the interconnectedness of energy and manifestation. At the fundamental level, everything in the universe is made up of energy. So, by aligning our energy with the reality we desire, we not only heal our physical, subtle, and higher being, but we also create a magnetic force that attracts and manifests that very reality into our lives.

You may have heard, "Your energy introduces you before you even speak." This beautifully encapsulates the importance of paying close attention to your energetic output. It emphasizes the power our energy has and how it influences our interactions and experiences in life. When we engage in energy clearing and alignment practices, we radiate a positive and magnetic energy that draws opportunities and manifestations toward us, and in turn, our energy becomes our powerful introduction to the world, before a word is spoken. Such energy showcases our readiness to live out our fullest potential.

Now, in case you are thinking, *Marie, I'm not sure about all this energy stuff. I need some evidence*, no problem! I am not here to sell you "woo-woo." I am all about looking deeper into anything recommended, to ensure it is solid.

Debunking the idea that energy healing, chakra work, and manifestation activities are "woo-woo" requires a deeper understanding of the scientific and experiential evidence supporting these practices. So, here are some key points to consider:

- Energy healing, chakra work, and manifestation activities are grounded in the principles of quantum physics which suggest that everything in the universe is composed of energy. Numerous scientific studies have shown that energy can be influenced and shifted, both within and around the human body. Practices like reiki, acupuncture, and mindfulness meditation have been shown to have measurable positive effects on physical and mental wellbeing. (More on quantum leaping in a later chapter.)
- The placebo effect, which is widely recognized in scientific research, shows how powerful belief, intention, and suggestion are in influencing health outcomes. Clearly, the mind has a profound impact on physical health. It is therefore perfectly reasonable to state that practices that promote relaxation, stress reduction, and positive thinking can enhance overall wellbeing.
- Countless individuals have shared their personal experiences of profound healing and transformation through energy healing, chakra work, and manifestation practices with me. While personal anecdotes are not considered scientific evidence, they provide valuable insight into the subjective experiences of individuals who have benefited from these practices. The sheer number of positive testimonials I have heard (including my own!) highlights the efficacy of these modalities.

- Many hospitals and healthcare centers now offer complementary and alternative therapies (CAM), including reiki, aromatherapy, and sound healing, alongside conventional treatments, to support holistic wellbeing. This demonstrates the growing acknowledgment of the value and effectiveness of these modalities.
- Energy healing, chakra work, and manifestation activities often incorporate mindfulness techniques which have been extensively studied and proven to reduce stress, improve mental health, and enhance overall quality of life. Mindfulness practices have gained widespread acceptance in fields such as psychology, education, and corporate wellness due to their scientifically documented benefits.

In sum, labeling energy healing, chakra work, and manifestation activities as "woo-woo" disregards the scientific research, experiential evidence, and integration into various domains of healthcare these modalities have seen over the years. While further research is still needed to fully understand the way the depths of how these modalities work, their potential for healing and transformation should not be dismissed. Open-mindedness and curiosity can lead to a deeper understanding and appreciation of these practices.

In the next chapter, we will delve deep into several practices that I have found to be both powerful and accessible for getting women to achieve greater alignment with the energetic frequencies that allow the universe to work with them. Before that, though, I want to introduce you to some more "basic" practices, starting with energy center alignment through your chakras.

Energy Center Alignment

Chakras, according to ancient Indian spiritual traditions, are energetic centers within the body that correspond to specific body parts, colors, and aspects of our being. Every thought and experience you have gets filtered through the chakra centers and the energy of that event is stored in the body. There are seven main chakras along the central channel of the body, from the crown of the head to the base of the spine. Oftentimes, the chakras are also referred to as energy wheels, which I think is a beautiful visual. As I describe the chakras, I invite you to place a hand on each of these energy centers on your body and visualize the color and energy of each one.

Here is a simplified explanation of each of the chakras. If you want to go deeper into this work, there are many wonderful books that focus solely on the chakra system, with detailed explanations on how to align them. This is also something I support clients with. I am always astounded by the shifts these clients have and how much more attuned they become to their own power and gifts after just one or two sessions!

- Root chakra (*Muladhara*). Located at the base of the spine, the root chakra is associated with the color red. It represents our foundation. It grounds us and offers a sense of security. When blocked, it can manifest as feelings of fear, anxiety, or instability. When it is clear and open, we experience a deep sense of safety, courage, and connection to the physical world. To strengthen this chakra, ask yourself, "What needs to be present for me to feel safe?" A lovely way to connect more with this center is to go outside, walk barefoot on the earth, place your hands on a tree, and feel the sun and breeze on your skin. Trust the messages that come through to you when you are in this state.

- Sacral chakra (*Svadhisthana*). The sacral chakra is situated in the lower abdomen (the "womb space" in women) and is associated with the color orange. It governs our creativity, passion, and sexuality, and when trauma has occurred, can often be traced to being held in this space. When this chakra is blocked, there is often a lack of inspiration, difficulty in expressing emotions, feeling "stuck", or issues with intimacy. By clearing and balancing the sacral chakra, you can unleash your creativity, embrace your sensuality, and cultivate healthier relationships. To support your sacral chakra, allow yourself to ponder, "What have I been longing to create more of in my life?" Do not hold back when answering this question.

- Solar plexus chakra (*Manipura*). Located in the upper abdomen, the solar plexus chakra is represented by the color yellow. It embodies personal power, self-esteem, and confidence. Blockages in this chakra may lead to low self-esteem, indecisiveness, or an excessive need for control. By clearing the solar plexus chakra, you can restore your inner strength, boost self-assurance, and manifest your desires with ease. When do you feel most aligned with your true power? Make a physical list of the times, places, people, situations, and experiences that support feelings of empowerment in you. Identify all the areas and circumstances in which you feel confident, resourceful, and capable. Look into ways you can bring these elements into the "blocked" areas of your life.

- Heart chakra (*Anahata*). The heart chakra, which is situated in the center of the chest, is associated with the color green. It governs your capacity to love, forgive, and experience compassion. Blockages in the heart chakra can manifest as feelings of resentment, emotional pain, or difficulty in forming meaningful connections. Clearing and opening the heart chakra allows for the experience of unconditional love, empathy, and deep emotional healing. While there are many ways to activate this chakra (such as a daily gratitude practice), one powerful question to ask yourself (and listen for your "higher self" answer for) is, "What do I feel has been missing from my life?" This may be a person, place, or thing. More often than not, it is a feeling, whether deep peace, unbounded love, full joy, or childlike excitement. Once you pinpoint what is missing, it will be easier for you to take inspired action to bring it closer.

- Throat chakra (*Vishuddha*). The throat chakra is located in the throat area and is represented by the color blue. It governs your ability to communicate, express yourself authentically, and speak your truth. Blockages in this chakra may lead to difficulties in expressing thoughts, fear of judgment, or a lack of effective communication. By clearing and aligning the throat chakra, you can find your authentic voice, enhance your communication skills, and express yourself with clarity and confidence. This chakra is one that has been blocked in many of the women I have worked with, so consider what may be stopping you from speaking your truth. It is also the chakra that holds the most influence over your ability to manifest your goals. This is because in order to manifest effectively, you need to be able to clearly state what you desire, what you do not desire, and the values you hold most dear. You may begin to clear this chakra by journaling, guided by the prompt, "What would I say if there was nothing or no one holding me back?"

- Third eye chakra (*Ajna*). Situated in the center of the forehead between the eyebrows, the third eye chakra is associated with the color indigo. It represents intuition, inner wisdom, and spiritual insight. A blocked third eye chakra can result in a lack of clarity, disconnection from intuition, or a feeling of being lost. By clearing this chakra, you can awaken your intuition, gain clarity, and access higher levels of consciousness. When you imagine your future life, what do you see? Be honest with yourself. Do you see barriers and roadblocks, or do you see a beautiful path before you? If you see struggles and challenges, pay extra-special attention to Chapter 5. Here, you will be guided in visualization practices in which you can use your third eye to envision yourself dismantling barriers before they even take physical form. Pretty cool, right?

- Crown chakra (*Sahasrara*). The crown chakra, which is located at the top of the head, is represented by the color violet or white. It connects you to the divine, universal consciousness and your highest self. Imbalances in the crown chakra can manifest as spiritual disconnection, closed-mindedness, or a lack of purpose. When you clear and open the crown chakra, you can experience spiritual awakening, connection, and a sense of purpose and meaning in your life. To start clearing your crown chakra, consider,

"If I knew without a doubt that I am abundantly supported, what would I create right now? Not in five years or ten years, but right now, beginning today?" Take a moment to write down what you desire to mold into reality and take inspired action!

Practices for Increased Alignment: Mindfulness

Mindfulness practices, such as meditation and yoga, can help foster a greater sense of awareness and presence in the moment. This can reduce fear and anxiety.

When we live in the present moment, we become more aware of our thoughts, feelings, and sensations. This can help us to recognize when we are feeling stressed or overwhelmed and to take steps to address these feelings before they become too big to deal with. It can also help us to recognize when we are feeling joy or contentment, so we can fully savor these experiences as they are unfolding. Savoring can boost our mood as it helps us to remember the good things that happen, keep us in the moment, and increase our gratitude, according to Dr. Laurie Santos, creator of The Science of Well-Being. Living in the present moment additionally improves our relationships with others, because when we are fully present with someone, we give them our full attention and listen deeply to what they are saying. This can help us to build deeper connections with our loved ones and to cultivate greater empathy and understanding.

Practicing mindfulness can feel challenging when you have a busy career or family life, but it is still possible to incorporate mindfulness practices into your daily routine. (It is also necessary, if you want to be able to receive messages from your future self.) Here are some tips for practicing mindfulness, even when you are busy:

- Start small. If you are new to mindfulness, start with just a few minutes of it each day. This could take the form of a daily five-minute mindfulness meditation before you start your day or go to bed at night. You can gradually increase the amount of time you spend in meditation as you become more comfortable with the practice.

- Set yourself reminders to take a few deep breaths or to check in with your body on your phone or computer. Use these moments as opportunities to cultivate awareness of the present moment and bring peace to the body.
- Integrate mindfulness into your daily activities. You do not have to set aside specific time for mindfulness practice if this is unrealistic for you. Instead, practice mindfulness when you are washing dishes, walking the dog, or commuting to work. Focus your attention on the present moment and fully engage in the activity.
- Practice self-compassion. It is important to be kind to yourself and to recognize that mindfulness is a journey. If you miss a day or feel like you are not making progress, do not give up. Be gentle with yourself and try again tomorrow.
- Use guided meditations. There are many wonderful apps and online resources that offer guided meditations for busy people. These meditations (which can be as short as five minutes) will help you to cultivate mindfulness in a structured and supportive way.

Remember, mindfulness is a daily practice, not something you master overnight. By incorporating mindfulness practices into your routine, even in small ways, you are cultivating greater awareness, reducing your stress, and improving your overall wellbeing. This is a win for your future self!

Meditation

Starting a regular meditation practice can be a little intimidating if you are new to it, but it doesn't have to be complicated. Simply:

- Choose a time when you are less likely to be interrupted.
- Find a quiet space where you will not be disturbed. This could be a spare room, a corner of your bedroom, or a spot in your backyard. Make sure the space is comfortable and free of distraction. If

possible, add personal touches that help remind you of your inner strength.

- Get into a comfortable position, either on a cushion or a chair. You do not have to sit cross-legged if that is not comfortable for you; you can sit on a chair with your back straight, your feet on the ground, and your hands resting in your lap.

- Close your eyes or soften your gaze and bring your attention to your breath. Notice the sensation of the breath as it enters and leaves your body. You might find it helpful to count your breaths, or to focus on the rise and fall of your chest.

- Make meditation a regular part of your routine, even just a couple minutes each day.

Your mind will inevitably wander during meditation practice, and that is okay. When you notice that your mind has wandered, gently bring your attention back to your breath. Do not judge yourself or get frustrated; this is a natural part of the practice.

Start with just a few minutes of meditation each day and remember that the goal is not to clear your mind of all thoughts, but to cultivate awareness and acceptance of the present moment.

In my early twenties, I found myself at a "happiness class" at a local Zen Buddhist community. By that point in my formal education, I had taken just about every type of class, but never one focused on happiness! That was the start of five magical years learning from and practicing with the *sangha* (community). I even moved to the center's property. Every day, I would wake up at 5:30AM to practice morning meditation, and every night, I would sit outside on a cushion in the quiet, firefly-lit dusk. This is also where I participated in and co-facilitated my first retreats.

When I first began meditating, I found it excruciatingly difficult. My legs would shake, my heart would race, and quite a few times, I even thought I was going to puke all over the shiny wooden floor as a golden Buddha sat watching me. Thank goodness I had a community to practice with. Otherwise, I likely would have walked out. I once tried to, in fact. However, the master teacher, Anton Somlai, pulled me aside and warned me that what I was feeling was toxic energy leaving my body. Years of fear, years of abuse, years of not living in peace, all the dust of anxiety and depression, was leaving my body. "Trust the process," he said, his eyes loving and gently encouraging. I did just that, and I swear it saved my life. I felt a noticeable bodily shift when I got into the swing of it, and my weekly migraines nearly subsided completely. To this day, I only get one or two per year. My breathing improved, and my childhood asthma disappeared. In the moments of deep pain and darkness that have come in the years since, I have still been able to see a glimmer of light, thanks to meditation. It has become a source of connection with my highest self. This practice is something that no one can take from me and that I cannot possibly be separated from, even if I someday stop meditating. Because of meditation, the relationship I have developed with my spirit is rock solid, so nothing has ever felt truly impossible or hopeless since then.

When I practiced at the Zen Center, there was not as much scientific research about the positive benefits of meditation as there is today. Most findings were anecdotal. Still, the master teacher (Anton), who had a PhD in psychology, was thrilled that the science was slowly starting to catch up to what the ancient teachers had known for centuries. Finally, there was growing academic acknowledgment of the fact that what looks like sitting and doing nothing on the outside allows the body to heal itself physically, mentally, energetically, and spiritually from the inside out.

Energetically Clearing Our Space

Energy cleansing rituals play a vital role in creating sacred spaces that nurture our growth, healing, and spiritual wellbeing. These rituals are designed to clear stagnant or negative energy from our physical surroundings, to allow positive and harmonious vibrations to flow freely. By consciously engaging in energy cleansing, we create an environment that supports us on all levels.

One powerful energy cleansing ritual is smudging. This involves burning sacred herbs, such as sage, palo santo, or sweetgrass, and using the smoke to cleanse the space. Before every retreat I lead, we cleanse the space together in a sacred ceremony. As the smoke ascends through the air, it acts as a purifying agent, clearing away dense or stagnant energy. This ritual of smudging can be done in any space, whether your home, office, or sacred gathering places. If you are concerned about your lungs or the smoke detector, you can also use a crystal, clearing spray, or even your intentions. So long as your intention is to reset the energetic atmosphere, any energy cleaning ritual can create a sense of freshness and renewal.

If you do choose to use sacred herbs, please be mindful of where you purchase your supplies from, so you can ensure the herbs are free of chemicals and so you can pay respect to the indigenous communities who have been using this sacred medicine for many lifetimes. Start your intentions with gratitude to those who have made the cultivation and use of these sacred plants possible.

Another popular energy cleansing ritual is the use of sound, such as bells, singing bowls, or chanting. Sound has a profound impact on the energetic vibrations of a space, and by using these tools, you can create sacred sounds that resonate with higher frequencies and disperse any lower vibrational energies. This ritual can be particularly effective when combined with a visualization of the soundwaves reverberating through the space, purifying and revitalizing it.

Crystals can also be used for energy cleansing. Crystals possess unique energetic properties that can absorb, transmute, and release stagnant or negative energies. By strategically placing crystals in your environment, you create an energetic grid that supports the cleansing and balancing of the space. Clear quartz, selenite, and black tourmaline are some examples of crystals that are commonly used for energy cleansing purposes, as these crystals amplify positive energy while dispelling negativity.

Energy cleansing rituals are not just about removing negative or stagnant energy. They go beyond that. They are sacred and intentional practices that allow us to connect with the inherent power of our intention and to co-create a space that aligns with our highest aspirations. By infusing our energy cleansing rituals with love, gratitude, and mindfulness, we elevate the entire process, infusing the space with positive intentions and blessings. In this scenario, we can connect more deeply with our intuition, creativity, and inner wisdom. Furthermore, these rituals help us to release accumulated stress, tension, and negative emotions, allowing us to enter a space of greater clarity, peace, and inspiration. As we cleanse the energy of our space, we also cleanse ourselves. Thus, the process becomes a sacred act of self-care, reminding us of the importance of tending to our energetic wellbeing. When we enter a purified and sacred space, we feel a sense of upliftment, tranquility, and expansion, and this allows us to flourish and thrive in all areas of our lives.

Over the past few years, I have greatly benefited from the genius of two women whose niche lies in creating harmonious environments. Funnily enough, both are also named Marie. The first is Marie Kondo, who is an organizing consultant, media host, and author widely known for her ability to "spark joy" in homes and offices. The second is Marie Diamond, a feng shui expert and transformational author. When I was first putting these women's principles into practice, I began with my bedroom. This room had always felt too open, the energy misaligned. After decluttering and tidying up KonMari style, I delved into Diamond's feng shui, rearranged furniture and artwork, and organized my space with my personal energy number in mind. The difference this made was incredible. Once complete, I immediately felt a shift in energy and a sense of calm and peace, and I now sleep better at night. The best part? This transformation did not cost a cent. It just took inspired action and an open mind!

Along with the two Maries, I look to Hestia, the ancient Greek Goddess of hearth, home, and family, for inspiration in this area. Hestia embodies warmth, hospitality, and sacred sanctuary, and she encourages us to nurture our wellbeing and cultivate a sense of comfort and belonging. By channeling the essence of these women and taking inspired action, I have manifested a home that is a sanctuary of tranquility, refuge, peace, and sacredness. You can do the same!

To create a peaceful environment that will support your journey and that is inspired by Hestia, Marie Kondo, and Marie Diamond, it is essential to prioritize simplicity. Strive to reduce clutter in your environment. Dispose of excess material possessions that may cause unnecessary distraction or stress. When your surroundings are disorganized, cluttered, or chaotic, this can create a sense of overwhelm and make it challenging for you to focus and maintain a sense of calm. I learned from my spiritual teachers, Anton (who you met earlier) and Linda Somlai, that a cluttered mind leads to a cluttered space, and a cluttered space leads to a cluttered mind. I have a lot of room for improvement here myself, but when my house is clean and organized (well, as much as it can be with three children!), the energy in my body feels so much freer and lighter, and my focus becomes supercharged.

Along with decluttering, consider infusing your home with beauty and nourishment. Surround yourself with natural elements like plants, flowers, and gentle lighting. Add scents that soothe and uplift your spirit, whether essential oils, incense, or fresh flowers. Curate a space that reflects your personal aesthetic and brings you joy. You may also want to learn more about feng shui and how this ancient practice can support a deeper level of balance, peace, and abundance in your home.

The environment you choose to be in has a profound impact on your energy and mindset. By consciously cultivating a nurturing and supportive environment, you invite the energies of growth, abundance, and manifestation into your life, and you create a space that nurtures your dreams and fuels your motivation to take meaningful action.

Decrease Demand and Increase Capacity

Stress and overwhelm happen when the demand for our energy, time, and resources outweighs our capacity to deliver them. Thus, if we want to be less stressed and more aligned, we must intentionally do two things: decrease demand and replenish energy.

To decrease demand, consider what you need to delete or delegate in your life. For example, let's say you have wanted to create an online course for years, but have never gotten the momentum to do it. If your heart is not fully in it, even if you feel you "should" do it, delete. A "should" goal without heart typically falls flat anyway. On the other hand, if that online course is something that you want to do with all of your heart but you just are not sure of the logistics on how to make it happen, delegate it! There are thousands of highly skilled professionals who can assist, from helping you with on-camera confidence to editing video footage to marketing the course, and they would be happy to use their divine gifts to help you share yours. If you keep trying to DIY it and it has been on your list for months (or even years), the financial investment of getting support will be well worth it from an energetic point of view. It will also contribute to your sense of confidence and self-trust. Additionally, can you delete hour-long conversations with long-distance relatives and offer a designated day and time to chat, to avoid random phone calls and back-to-back messages? Can you delegate household chores, such as cleaning and yard maintenance to other household members or professionals?

I once happened to be scrolling through comments on a video that highlighted a professional working woman doing chores. People from several other countries were appalled. I found out that day that in many countries, working women (especially if they have children) are expected to have paid help for cleaning, cooking, and errands. One commenter even joked that the maids have maids, because truly, no one can do everything themselves, nor should they be expected to. Where I am in the United States, however, it is more rare for a family to have this type of support, even if the family can afford it or desperately needs it. This is because so many of us were taught to believe that we must do it all ourselves. No wonder we are energetically overloaded! Some of the burden needs to be lifted off our shoulders before we collapse. You were not put on this planet to be a workhorse!

Now, let's turn to increasing capacity (or replenishing our energy). To do this, it is always essential to return to the basics: nutrition, sleep, movement, hydration, the words we fill our minds with, and the environment we are in. All these things have a significant impact on our physical, mental, and emotional energy. We can also increase our energy by increasing our knowledge and skills. Think about when you first learned how to do something—tying your shoes, for instance. When you were first learning, you probably felt frustrated as you tried again and again, using all your mental energy on this task. Once you mastered this skill, however, the task became effortless, therefore requiring no additional energy. The same can be said for every aspect of our lives. The more we know and the more we hone our skills, the easier and more effortless those tasks become. Putting in a little extra time and energy in learning and understanding a process can yield massive results in the long run.

Applying Energetic Upleveling

One of the most rewarding aspects of my journey has been the opportunities I have been given to facilitate healing circles and retreats. Here, women come together to initiate their own journeys of self-discovery and empowerment. These gatherings provide a safe and nurturing space for the participants to connect, share, and support one another. Through energy work, guided meditations, new adventures, and intentional rituals, we delve into the depths of our beings, shedding layers of conditioning and embracing our authentic selves. In these sacred spaces, we create a supportive and nurturing environment that allows for deep healing, spiritual connection, and the exploration of our highest purpose. We give one another the gift of being seen, heard, and honored in our most vulnerable moments.

The work I do draws upon ancient wisdom that has withstood the test of time. In a world that often feels fragmented and disconnected, we are awakening to the truth that our wellbeing is intricately intertwined with the wellbeing of Mother Gaia (Earth) and all other beings.

Modern society may offer us countless conveniences and advancements, but we cannot ignore the cost at which these advancements come. Our health (physical, mental, and spiritual) has suffered as we have become disconnected from ourselves, each other, and the natural world. The call to return to ancient wisdom has never been stronger. This is why many of these traditions, which took a backseat to contemporary medicine for decades, are now becoming mainstream. Twenty to thirty years ago, it was rare to hear of women (especially professional women) practicing yoga and reiki, exploring Goddess lineages, and traveling to sacred destinations around the world to explore the local medicine and wisdom there. It is my mission to support women in clearing their path and to empower them to step into their highest purpose and live lives of authenticity, joy, and fulfillment. Together, women of all backgrounds are reclaiming our birthright as powerful beings of light. We are forging a new path that integrates the ancient with the modern and where the soul meets the science. We are creating a future where healing and wholeness form the core of our existence.

Goddess Inspiration: Isis (Magic and Intuition)

The Egyptian Goddess Isis is the luminous embodiment of magic, intuition, and divine wisdom. Commonly depicted with her wings outstretched, Isis symbolizes the expansiveness of intuition and the ability to soar beyond the limits of the physical world. When you intentionally draw from her mystical energy and tap into her intuitive wisdom, you become able to recognize your innate connection to the unseen realms. You may also discover practices that enhance your intuitive abilities or find yourself stepping into leadership roles, whether in your career, relationships, or personal endeavors, leading with compassion, wisdom, and a deep sense of responsibility for the wellbeing of those you serve. With Isis by your side, you can become a catalyst for positive change, leaving a lasting impact on those around you.

Just as Isis leans into the mysteries of the cosmos, trust in your own inner "knowing" and the guidance of your intuition. As you attune yourself to the vibrations of the unseen, you will find that synchronicities and signs become guideposts along your journey.

Have you ever felt, seen, or heard whispers from the universe that seemed to come just at the right time? Maybe you have even had moments of déjà vu, where you could swear that you have already lived the experience you are currently having. These moments are not accidental; they are a divine gift. So often, we push them away, thinking that they must not be real or that we are imagining things. Maybe we were even told as children that magic is not real, and so we pushed our intuition deep, burying it under everyone else's opinions, beliefs, and ideas of how we should live our lives. No more! There are several ways in which you can (re)connect with your intuition and embody Isis's essence.

One is clairvoyance, or "clear seeing". An example of clairvoyance would be a situation where you are drawn to two life coaches and are not sure which one to hire. When you look at them, one may appear to be "illuminated." This is clairvoyance. It is you clearly seeing how your energy interacts with their energy. The other coach may be an amazing woman who helps many, but you just do not feel the same pull toward her as you do the first.

Another method of intuitive reconnection is clairsentience, or "clear sensation/clear feeling". This is experienced as an undeniable feeling in the body. Let's say that while you are booking a vacation, a sudden feeling of dread forms in your gut (this is where the phrase "trust your gut" comes into play) and you can feel a drop in your energy. This could be an instance of clairsentience, and such moments should be paid close attention to. Do not be trigger happy with how you respond to these moments, though, as this could be a mind-based fear, not your future self. We will be talking about this in more detail in the next chapter.

Fun fact: while this mind-gut connection has been known in spiritual communities for ages, science is also now proving that our brain and gut are in constant communication through a special connection called the gut-brain axis. This link influences your emotions, decision-making, and even your intuition. So, when you have a "gut feeling" about something, it could be your inner wisdom speaking to you. Trust those instincts! While it may not always have a clear explanation, it can guide you in making better choices.

A third way in which you can connect to your intuition is clairaudience, or "clear hearing." "Trust your inner voice" is a popularized phrase that gives a nod to clairaudience. Have you ever thought you heard guidance from within, or even from someone close that had passed away? If not, that is okay; you likely receive guidance in other forms. If you have, did you pay attention? Did you open your heart and allow yourself to receive and get curious about the message? Some people can hear their intuition as if a friend is whispering into their ear.

When you lean into Isis's influence and embrace moments of clairvoyance, clairsentience, and clairaudience, you discover that magic is not just an external force, but a reflection of your own inner power. Whether this is your first time stepping into trusting your highest wisdom or you are a fully-fledged mantra-chanting, kirtan-singing, oracle-card-pulling, crystal-cleansing, full-moon-drumming sister (or dance somewhere in between), I promise that when you ask your highest self to allow this book to bring you what you need at this time, you will see, feel, or hear exactly what you need to know.

Inspired Action

If I could inspire you to take one action today, I would ask for you to add five minutes of intentional stillness into your calendar. If you need to remove something from your schedule to make that happen, do it! Five minutes of quiet, stillness, and presence brings innumerable blessings. When you want to quit, think of me with a gentle, loving smile, saying, "Trust the process." I love the mantra, "Present moment. Only moment."

This can be said repeatedly, anywhere, anytime. When you know this to be true, there is no fear.

If you already incorporate stillness into your daily routine, then perfect! Keep going.

I also invite you to take out a journal or a notebook and write what comes up for you when you read this quote:

Our deepest fear is not that we are inadequate. Our deepest fear is that we are powerful beyond measure. It is our light, not our darkness, that most frightens us. We ask ourselves, "Who am I to be brilliant, gorgeous, talented, fabulous?"
—Marianne Williamson

If you feel uncomfortable sensations in your body or mind as you read this, breathe through it. Acknowledge these sensations. Then, come back to the present moment. I encourage you to not run or hide, but to work through this feeling and keep writing, even if it means starting and stopping several times to regulate your nervous system. It is when we learn to be the observer of our emotions rather than the victim of them that we unveil the confidence within and learn that we can trust ourselves.

If you would like a five-minute guided meditation from me to restore alignment, go to www.goddessoflightretreats.com/meditation. This would be a great starting point for your inspired action for this chapter.

Align

3

ALIGN WITH COURAGE

_____

Nothing in life is to be feared, it is only to be understood. Now is the time to
understand more, so that we may fear less.

—attributed to Marie Curie

A LLOW ME TO SHARE WITH YOU the inspiring story of Jen, a woman who had always dreamed of traveling the world and immersing herself in new experiences.

Jen's heart longed for the thrill of exploring different cultures and the breathtaking beauty of diverse landscapes. However, the thought of booking her own travels and venturing into the unknown by herself overwhelmed her. Doubt and fear held her back. For years, she sat with an unstamped passport in hand, waiting for the courage to book a flight.

One fortunate day, Jen came across my Goddess of Light Destination retreats. As she read about the luxurious retreat I was planning in the enchanting paradise of Costa Rica, her heart skipped a beat. The retreat offered what she had dreamed of: ziplining through the lush jungle; horseback riding on pristine beaches; indulgence in gourmet meals prepared on-site. It was as if the trip had been tailored precisely to her desires. With a mix of excitement and trepidation, Jen reached out to inquire about the retreat. The allure was undeniable, but she had a moment of hesitation; could she truly step outside her comfort zone and leap heart first into this enchanting adventure? The prospect of traveling alone to a new place felt daunting.

Jen voiced her concerns to me, and I listened compassionately. I could understand the swirling emotions she was experiencing all too well as I've had similar thoughts in the past. I reassured her that her fears were natural and valid. Together, we explored her hesitations, acknowledging them without allowing them to dictate her actions.

Often when we are ready to say yes to something new, the mind says, "Wait! I have never done this before. How do I know I will be okay?" and looks for reasons out. It's our ego's way to keep us safe, so it believes, but it's usually not in our best interest because it keeps us stuck in fear and old stories. To override this process, we must allow ourselves to breathe through the nerves and listen to our heart.

Jen chose to trust herself enough to leap forward. Despite the fear, doubt, and overwhelm that threatened to hold her back, she knew deep down that if she did not make this choice now, her dream would remain nothing more than that, and that she would have to live with regret. Jen exclaimed, "Let's do it!" and reserved her space at the retreat.

As she did so, a mixture of excitement and uncertainty coursed through Jenny's veins. The thrill of knowing that she had entrusted herself with the opportunity to make this wildly passionate desire a reality was both exhilarating and nerve-wracking. The journey to Costa Rica represented more than just a physical trip for Jen; it was a voyage of self-discovery, empowerment, and awakening.

In the months leading up to the retreat I recommended visualization practices and positive affirmations for Jen to do. I reminded her that she was not alone on this journey; that the retreat would be a sanctuary of support, connection, and growth.

During the retreat, something new awoke inside of her as she discovered her tribe, developed true, loving friendships with the other women (who just a week prior had been strangers), courageously flew through the jungles via zipline, and ran through the sands to splash in the ocean with the enthusiasm of a young girl. When I led the group through a powerful guided meditation after we returned from this retreat of a lifetime, she proclaimed through tears, "I feel like my life is just beginning!"

Jen's story speaks to the power of self-trust and taking inspired action. By trusting herself and choosing to step forward, she began the process of transcending her limitations. Jen now carries within her a newfound sense of courage and determination. She has embraced the belief that if she steps into courage and casts aside fear and doubts, she allows herself the opportunity to live her life to the fullest.

The Undercurrents of Fear

Fear is pain in the anticipation of pain. Fear is an emotion that creates a disconnect from the present moment. The only way to overcome it is to see it for what it is, then move through it.

Like in Jen's case, we often experience breakdowns before the breakthroughs happen. These cannot and should not be avoided. I once heard that an experiment was done in which trees were grown in an isolated environment that had no wind, to determine if the trees would survive better in a less volatile climate. What happened was the exact opposite: the trees grew to be weak and brittle. As a result, the researchers acknowledged that it was the force of the winds that made the trees strong, resilient, and able to withstand incredible pressure. We are much the same. To be "resilient" means to "spring back." How do we spring back, or become resilient, if there is never any pressure? It is the sudden release of pressure that makes a coil leap high. Do you remember playing with a toy when you were young that you had to press down, then it sprung up high into the air causing you to laugh in amazement of this simple yet incredible feat? However, we unfortunately tend to resist what can help us rise up, because we believe in the fear that comes with hardship more than we believe in our own power to spring back. I for one am ready to watch you in amazement as you elevate!

Identifying the source of a fear or a breakdown can be a challenging task, especially when the fear is deeply rooted in past experiences. Childhood trauma, for instance (which can include physical, sexual, and emotional abuse, neglect, or exposure to violence), has been found to be a significant source of fear for many people (myself included). In fact, research has shown that people who experienced childhood trauma are more likely to develop anxiety and other mental health issues later in life. This is significant, because I have yet to meet a woman who has not been a victim of emotional, financial, physical, sexual, or spiritual abuse at some point in her life. I shared a piece of my personal story of navigating trauma and learning how to thrive in *Powerhouse Women: Survivor to Thriver*, a compilation of the stories of several incredible female leaders who chose to no longer be victims of abuse and to create the lives of their dreams. (All proceeds go to non-profit organizations that support women who are also on the road from victimhood to survival to thriving, because safety and support during the healing process is essential.)

My story goes like this: I grew up with an abusive father, and I craved positive female empowerment. As I grew older, I feared that my traumatic history would hold me back from achieving my dreams of making a positive difference in the world. I was so afraid of messing up that I often would not speak or take advantage of opportunities that could be very beneficial to me. I had a persistent fear that I was not "enough"—not good enough, not smart enough, not wealthy enough, not pretty enough, not thin enough. As time went by and I leaned into the strategies we are exploring in this book, I discovered that *I am* enough—more than enough—one step at a time. As I embraced this truth, I also slowly realized that I could design my own destiny in many ways. From there, I have continued to find mountaintops that I can share this truth from, so that you (and countless other women who crave this change) can hear it, too.

My journey was not easy, and I was nervous to share my story, unsure of whether I could be a role model. However, my "why" of wanting to help others allowed me to stay motivated. I had a light that I followed, and by forging through my worries, I helped others find their spark. When women stay connected to their light—to their "why" and to their highest self—magic happens. Fear dissolves and is replaced with love and inspiration.

If the mention of trauma stirs something in you, whether a feeling, a memory, or a flashback, take a deep breath and allow it to move through and out. Take another deep breath and remind yourself that you are not alone. The healing that occurs from this space can help you move mountains. Rather than pushing these fears down, I encourage you to seek support, so you can allow this energy to be released and transmuted. This support may look like traditional therapy, intentional somatic movement, healing retreats, creative practices, or sound journeys. If one avenue does not resonate, I urge you to not give up and to continue connecting with healing modalities until one or more allows you to release your shame, blame, and self-judgment. Remember, healing is a process, not an overnight fix.

Along with the effects of childhood trauma, women often have a challenging time believing in themselves due to societal expectations and gender roles. Women tend to underestimate their abilities and accomplishments, leading to a vicious cycle of self-doubt, fear of failure, and procrastination. Mel Robbins, a motivational speaker and author, once said, "Procrastination is not a time management problem, it's an emotion management problem." In other words, procrastination, or always putting things off, is often a result of fear or anxiety. Addressing the underlying emotion is crucial if we are to overcome it.

If you are stuck in this space, remember that you have the power to control your destiny. Stay connected to your "why" and to your light, knowing that you can achieve your personal legend. It may not be easy, but with determination and self-belief, anything is possible. As Mel Robbins says, "You are one decision away from a completely different life." Not to mention, when you stay in fear, your body undergoes a series of physiological changes that can have negative effects on your health and wellbeing. Some of the ways fear can impact your body include:

- Stress response. When you are afraid, whether it is from perceived fear or intuitive fear (more on that in a moment), your body activates its stress response (also known as the "fight, flight, freeze, or fawn" response). This response triggers the release of stress hormones like cortisol and adrenaline. When you are exposed to these chemicals for an unnaturally long period of time, a variety of physical symptoms can manifest, including increased heart rate, rapid breathing, and muscle tension.

- Immune system suppression. Prolonged fear can suppress the immune system, leaving you more vulnerable to illness and disease. Your body was not designed to be in a constant state of stress and fear, so dis-ease is often the result.

- Digestive problems. Fear can cause digestive problems such as stomach pain, diarrhea, and nausea. I, for one, knew I needed to pay closer attention to my own stress management when these symptoms showed up unexpectedly in my life. Thousands of dollars' worth of medical bills later, no test could show anything wrong with me internally. It was only when I chose my health and wellbeing over my previous job that *all* the symptoms miraculously disappeared.

- Sleep disruption. Fear can disrupt your sleep patterns, making it difficult for you to fall or stay asleep. Getting less than seven hours of sleep a night can lead to weight management challenges, poor skin, and difficulty in regulating mood. Getting the right amount of quality sleep is truly your best friend.

- Mental health issues. Prolonged fear can lead to mental health issues, such as anxiety and depression. Please do not attempt to go through these things alone, should they appear in your life. There are amazing experts who can support you if you are struggling. Even a good virtual therapist can give you tools that can help you climb out of the hole. Time outside in nature and a regular workout routine can also do wonders in elevating your mental health.

Assess where you are now. Have you been in an elevated state of stress for more than a week? Are you consistently not getting at least seven hours of good quality sleep? Are you frequently becoming agitated with others, especially those you spend most of your time with? Take an honest look into what in your life does not feel aligned with joy, love, and ease. When you have identified what is out of alignment, you will have the insight needed to create something different. The moment I realized that I was the co-creator of my life and not simply a bystander, my entire world shifted.

Mind-Based Fear vs Intuitive Fear

If we are to align with courage, we first need to differentiate between the self-limiting fears we should overcome and the self-protecting fears that indicate real danger and should be respected.

Mind-based fear typically arises not from immediate danger but from internal sources, such as self-limiting beliefs, past experiences, or imagined negative outcomes. It often pops up when you are stepping out of your comfort zone, trying new things, or facing situations where the outcome is uncertain (but not necessarily harmful). Key characteristics include:

- Anxiety. This fear is often irrational and based on anxiety or overthinking (rather than actual risk).
- Growth inhibiting. It prevents personal growth and development because it keeps you from taking actions that could lead to positive change or beneficial opportunities. Remember, your ego wants to keep you from changing because it does not understand the unknown.

Common examples of mind-based fears are public speaking, failure, and rejection. In these examples, the risk is more about discomfort than danger.

Overcoming this type of fear usually involves rational thinking, subconscious reprogramming, exposure, and confidence building. The emphasis is on recognizing the fact that fear itself is the barrier, not any real external threat.

In contrast to mind-based fear, intuitive fear is an instinctive response that serves as a protective mechanism. This type of fear is tied to your survival instincts and tends to appear quickly in response to actual dangers. It should generally be trusted and acted upon. Key characteristics include:

- Rooted in instinct. This fear is an instinctive reaction to immediate threat, and often feels visceral or gut-driven. This is where the phrase "trust your gut" comes into play.
- Protective. Its primary function is to keep you safe by alerting you to danger and motivating you to take immediate action.

Intuitive fear might occur if you are walking down a dark alley. In this situation, fear may manifest as a sudden feeling of unease. As another example, perhaps you once met someone who seemed outwardly friendly but who made you feel uncomfortable for reasons you could not pinpoint. This is intuitive fear coming into play. With these fears, you have a strong sense that something is "off".

Understanding these two types of fear can help you to better recognize when to push your boundaries (such as in Jen's case above) and when to heed a warning for your physical, emotional, or spiritual safety. Mind-based fear can be overcome; intuitive fear should be carefully considered and respected (remember what we said in the previous chapter about paying attention to clairvoyance, clairsentience, and clairaudience).

As a starting point, mind-based fear will often feel confusing and unsettling. You may be excited one moment and then want to run in the opposite direction the next, when things start to feel too big or overwhelming. In contrast, intuitive, gut-based fear will often persist and even expand if it is ignored. Telling the difference between these two fears can sometimes be challenging, but a few tips can help:

1. Assess the source. Reflect on whether your fear is coming from inside (anxiety about what might happen based on past experience or imagined futures) or from something in your immediate environment that poses a real threat.

2. Examine the evidence. Look for tangible evidence that supports the legitimacy of the fear. Is there a clear and present danger, or are you worried about a possibility that is not fully grounded in reality?

3. Listen to your body. Notice your physical reactions. Intuitive fear tends to trigger intense physical responses linked to the body's acute stress response. For me, this often manifests as a jolt in my body or a "closing" sensation around my heart chakra.

4. Community support. Sometimes, discussing your fear with those you trust can help clarify whether you are facing a legitimate concern or a harmless personal anxiety. You may be surprised to find that when you share a red-flag concern with someone, they had the same exact feeling, and you both are now affirmed that this is a genuine concern.

I want to share with you some of the practices that changed my life and allowed me to not only overcome the breakdowns, panic attacks, and self-doubt that came with my mind-based fears, but that also elevated my mindset and my way of being to the point where I am now confident in who I am and how I help. These practices allow me to live a life that deeply aligns with my core values, beliefs, and desires.

When I dare to be powerful, to use my strength in the service of my vision,
then it becomes less and less important whether I am afraid.
—Audre Lorde

Journaling

Keeping a journal is *not* just for your teenage daughter! Journaling is a powerful tool that can help you process your thoughts and emotions, gain clarity and perspective, improve your mental and emotional wellbeing, and step into the courage your future-self harbors. By incorporating journaling into your routine (even in small ways), you can gain a greater sense of clarity and self-awareness and move closer to your goals and aspirations. Writing is medicine that opens the doorway to communication with your soul.

The benefits of journaling include:

- Reduced stress. Writing down your thoughts and emotions can help to reduce stress and anxiety, as it allows for the release of pent-up emotions and for a sense of clarity and control.

- Increased self-awareness. Journaling can help you become more aware of your patterns of thought and behavior. This will allow you to identify areas for growth and change.

- Boost in creativity. Writing can stimulate your creativity and imagination, helping you to generate new ideas and insights. (You will definitely need this as you create your dream life!)

- Improved problem-solving. Journaling can help you gain perspective on problems or challenges you may be facing. This can help you to approach them with a clearer and more focused mindset.

- Enhanced mood. Writing about positive experiences or things you are grateful for helps to boost your mood and sense of wellbeing.

- Increased confidence. When you write to release your fears and to manifest your desires, it gives you the extra momentum you need to move in the direction of your highest self.

To maximize the benefits of journaling, expressive writing may be the way to go. Social psychologist James W. Pennebacker discovered that expressive writing, especially writing "confessions" (i.e. things that worry you, what you are holding back, and painful experiences) is highly therapeutic. Allowing yourself fifteen minutes a day of expressive writing for only four consecutive days can reduce depression, anxiety, and physical pain and improve memory and sleep quality for up to six months. Now that is something worth writing about!

To quickly debunk a common misconception about expressive writing: writing about your fears will not manifest them, unless you keep going back to ruminate on them. Transfer those worries from your mind to your pen to the paper, and then burn it, baby—or rip it up and throw it in the trash. This ritual will signal to your mind and the universe that you are making space for greater things.

Even if you do not have a lot of free time or do not enjoy writing, there are still ways to incorporate journaling into your routine. Here are some tips:

- Just as with mindfulness, set aside a few minutes each day. This can make a big difference. Try to make it a consistent part of your routine, such as in the morning or before bed.

- Try using prompts. These can be as simple as, "How am I feeling today? What am I grateful for? What fears need to be released? What is holding me back from my goal? What do I crave more of in my life?"

- Try different formats. You do not have to write long, detailed entries to benefit from journaling. Try making bullet points lists or even drawings or doodles to capture your thoughts and emotions. Making it fun will inspire you to commit to the practice. Use coloring pencils or pastels, if you feel called to.

- Focus on the process, not the outcome. Remember that the goal of journaling is not to create a perfect piece of writing, but to explore your thoughts and emotions. Do not worry about spelling or grammar; just write what comes to mind. If you start writing without thinking or your handwriting even changes and it feels like you are not directly writing what flows onto the paper, congratulations! Your inner guidance has taken over and is helping you to see a new perspective. This is your intuitive, inner self sending you a message.

If you want to go even deeper into this practice, Julia Cameron recommends a daily practice called "morning pages" in her book *The Artist's Way*. This practice involves writing three pages of longhand stream-of-consciousness first thing in the morning. This can help to quiet our inner critic and fears and to access our deeper thoughts and desires. Here is a snippet from *The Artist's Way* that speaks into the power of journaling in overcoming fears:

> *As you move toward a dream, the dream moves toward you. To trust in yourself is to trust in the source that created you. And so you must trust your process, your vision, and your ability to create. All of these things are grounded in a deep, abiding faith in yourself.*

By using journaling as a tool to connect with our inner selves, we can gain the confidence and clarity needed to move past our fears and pursue our dreams, and to therefore lean fully into our highest selves.

Somatic Healing

So much of the trauma and hardships we experience cannot be processed through talk therapy. While I am an advocate for traditional therapy in many cases (such as for processing grief, learning nonviolent communication strategies, and learning tools to manage burnout), modalities such as somatic healing are often neglected altogether in favor of talk therapy, with dire consequences. We are not taught how to rewire our nervous system, process traumas that we can or cannot name, or discharge tension. All of this can be done through somatic healing.

We begin to form memories in our nervous system while we are still in the womb. During this time, we can form traumatic memories that we do not even have the language to understand, much less consciously recall. Our cognitive intellect makes up only a fraction of our total wisdom, and, quite frankly, the more we try to understand something cognitively, the more confusion and anxiety we may end up with.

As Brooke Yantzi, founder of Dance Alchemy, explains, "Embodied transformation [somatic healing] allows us to be in response to our environment, rather than react." In other words, it allows us to be intentional about how we act. "Reactions" comes from our unhealed stories, which are trapped within the nervous system, so we can widen the gap between our experience of something and our response to it through appropriate boundaries, grounding and centering practices, connection to community, and co-regulation.

One of the most joyful and powerful ways I have experienced the release and transmuting of emotions is through Dance Alchemy. This natural medicine moves participants through the five elements of earth, water, fire, air, and ether, so they can deeply connect with and be present in their bodies, release and let go, feel greater freedom, expand what is possible, and come home to themselves, all while enjoying a sense of playfulness and flow within a community of others. Something beyond magical happens in this intentional movement space where sacred release and connection occurs. It's as if the doors to your soul open and you can see and feel exactly what your highest self needs you to in that moment (even if you have two left feet!).

Intentions

An intention is a focused statement that reflects your deepest desires and aspirations and that sets the course for your life. It becomes the programming of your mind. By setting clear intentions that are grounded in your values and beliefs, you can create a life that is rich with meaning, joy, and fulfillment. Setting intentions can also be a powerful way to overcome fear and doubt, as it allows us to focus our energy and attention on the things that we truly desire, rather than on our fears and worries.

Take a moment to reflect on your heart's deepest desires and set an intention that reflects your unique path and purpose in life. I encourage you to write these down. Trust that as you focus your energy and attention on your intentions, the universe conspires to support you in manifesting your dreams. This is the beginning of the co-creation process.

If you are stuck, here are some suggestions for you, dear Goddess:

- I intend to live a life of purpose and passion.

- I intend to pursue my dreams with courage and determination.
- I intend to embrace a mindset of growth and abundance.
- I intend to trust in myself and my abilities.
- I intend to take bold and inspired action toward my goals.
- I intend to surround myself with positivity and support, letting go of my attachment to relationships and situations that no longer serve me.
- I intend to be open and receptive to new opportunities and experiences.
- I intend to follow my intuition and inner guidance.

By setting these intentions, having a clear focus on your goals, and instilling a commitment to living a life of purpose and passion, you can overcome fear and doubt and create the life that you truly desire. Once you fully embody and believe the intention statement you have created, you can remove the "I intend" part and simply state (for example), "I live a life of purpose and passion."

Gratitude Practice

Imagine giving a friend a lovely gift—a home, a car, a job, a birdsong, a sunset, your favorite pumpkin spiced chai—and the friend never says thank you. Maybe they even keep asking for more, scoffing at the gifts you have already given them. Do you think you would ever want to go out of your way to give them gifts again? Well, it works the same with universal or divine blessings. Are you grateful for all the blessings, big and small, that come your way? Or are you dismissing what has been provided by claiming you never get what you want?

It is essential to express gratitude for what you already have. If you are unable to do that, it is unlikely you will keep receiving, and even if you do, you will always be in a state of perceived "lack", even if exactly what you once dreamed about is right in front of you.

By taking time each day to focus on what you are grateful for, you can cultivate greater appreciation for the blessings in your life, develop a more optimistic outlook, and send a message to the universe that says you do not take its blessings for granted.

One way to start a gratitude practice is to set aside a few minutes each day to write down three things you are grateful for. These could be big or small, simple or complex. The important thing is to truly feel gratitude for each thing on the list. Keep a small journal by your bed or use a gratitude app on your phone for this purpose. Many of these apps even allow you to upload photos. If you are struggling to come up with three things on a tough day, look back at your previous entries and bask in the gratitude from a day that felt fulfilling. This can change your current outlook and frequency.

Another powerful way to practice gratitude is to express it verbally, by telling loved ones or coworkers how much you appreciate them and why. When my brother passed away, I entered a deep state of regret over the fact that I had never told him how grateful I was to him for all the laughter and memories we shared; for how we were there for each other in a way that can never be replaced. Since I can no longer verbally tell him how grateful I am for these things, I sometimes say, "Thank you," (remember the *Ho'oponopono* prayer from Chapter 1) and think of all the reasons why I was grateful to have him in my life. Sometimes, I write to him in a journal to express my gratitude for him.

To make gratitude a habit, incorporate it into your daily routine. Set a reminder on your phone or incorporate it into your established morning or bedtime ritual. With consistent practice, you will find that gratitude becomes a natural and effortless part of your life and that it brings more joy and abundance into each day.

Goddess Inspiration: Sekhmet (Courage and Protection)

In the ancient Egyptian pantheon, the fierce and powerful Goddess Sekhmet reigns as a symbol of strength, protection, and divine justice. If you want to manifest power, courage, and fierce determination in your everyday life, this Goddess can serve as a profound inspiration for you.

One of Sekhmet's primary symbols is a lioness. This represents her fierce and resilient nature. Lions are known for their courage, fearlessness, and leadership. Taking inspiration from Sekhmet, you can lean into our own inner lioness, summoning the courage to confront difficult situations and stand up for what you believe in. Just as Sekhmet fearlessly protected and defended the divine order, you, too, can find the strength within yourself to face adversity head on as you take inspired action for your plans.

Sekhmet possessed the dangerous ability to unleash destructive power when angered. This shows the importance of us channeling our strength responsibly and wisely. It teaches us to cultivate self-control and balance paired with harnessing our courage and power for our highest good.

In our society, women are discouraged from expressing anger, and when we do, it can be seen as mentally unstable, childish, aggressive, irrational, or overly sensitive. If you are a woman of color, the judgment you face for this is often even greater. Why is it that the male human is, culturally and historically, allowed to get angry without much fear of retribution, while women are demonized for expressing anger? Maybe because, many moons ago, men learned that a woman's rage had the power to deconstruct worlds and it left them terrified. We do not get angry over nothing though, do we, sister? No. When someone continues to take advantage of our loving kindness, when someone causes harm to our babies or loved ones, when we are exploited for money, when we have our human rights taken from us, that is when we become enraged. The force of a woman's emotion (energy in motion) can move mountains. When angered, we are unstoppable. This power was terrifying to the men who wanted to control the minds, actions, and freedoms of our ancestors, so they created new norms and standards for how women should speak, behave, think, and even dress through religious expectations and government laws. Society was built around forcing us into submission, and unfortunately, there are millions, honestly billions, of people around the planet who are still confined to these man-made expectations. But as each of us speaks up and out, the collective becomes more free.

To embody the power of Sekhmet's transformative energy, allow yourself to get angry. Scream, yell, growl, and howl at the moon! We have centuries and centuries of pent-up anger inside us that has been passed down from our grandmothers, and their grandmothers, and their grandmothers, and we are in a unique time in history where we are safer than we have been for dozens of generations to transmute this exceptionally potent emotion of anger into a force that can catalyze real and lasting positive change in the world. This begins with each one of us giving ourselves permission to get angry about the harm and injustice we have faced, and to not care what anyone else will think of us for it.

Many women (especially those who were born before the tech boom) believe that if they express their anger, they will disrupt peace and harmony. However, the opposite is true. When there is quiet unrest lying under the surface, this ultimately festers into frustration, and then explosive anger. Alternatively, when we can acknowledge and take action on what is making our blood boil, true change can happen, and this gives others the courage to stand up, too. Consider Rosa Parks, Susan B. Anthony, Frida Kahlo, Gloria Steinem, Sojourner Truth, Malala Yousafzai, Tarana Burke, Angela Davis, Winona LaDuke, and Waris Dirie (to name just a few). These women refused to hold their rage inside any longer and channeled it into movements, advocacy, books, and nonprofits to bring more racial equality, gender equality, women's rights, and environmental protection to the forefront of our social consciousness, so we could take collective inspired action and make much-needed changes.

Connecting with Sekhmet's energy means exploring our own emotions and vulnerabilities in this way. She symbolizes the power to overcome inner turmoil and emerge stronger. In our daily lives, we can embody this by taking the time to acknowledge and process our fears, doubts, and insecurities, gaining a deeper understanding of ourselves and cultivating the inner resilience necessary to face challenges. When we draw inspiration from her and embody these qualities in our everyday lives, we summon the lioness within us, fearlessly facing challenges and standing up for what we believe in. By tempering our strength with wisdom and self-control, we can use our power constructively.

Inspired Action

Intentional journaling can open doors into unconscious thought patterns and incredible messages from your higher self. Download this list of free journaling prompts at www.goddessoflightretreats.com/prompts before you move onto the next chapter.

4

THE PROMISES WE MAKE TO OURSELVES

———

The Goddess falls in love with Herself, drawing forth her own emanation,
which takes on a life of its own. Love of self for self is the creative force of the
universe.

—Starhawk

I HAVE AN ANNUAL PLANNER THAT begins the year with a page titled, "My promise to myself this year." As I reread what I journalled in this section at the start of this year, I feel a sense of joy washing over me. It is like a blueprint for how I desire to move through life.

I will tell you in a moment what I have previously included in these promises, but first, I want to be very clear on why making self-promises (and following through on them) is one of the most important things you can do for yourself if you are to live a life of purpose on your own terms.

While it is important to keep your promises to others, there is one person that depends on you being true to your word more than anyone else on the planet. It is not your partner, parents, children, team, employees, employers, or clients. The promises you make to *yourself* are the most important ones you will ever keep. When you do not make good on your word to yourself, you lose trust in yourself, and when you lose trust in yourself, you lose confidence, lack motivation, and do not believe that what you desire is truly achievable. You may even stop setting big goals altogether. To add insult to injury, when you do not keep your promises to yourself, it is nearly impossible for others to fully trust you. We show others how to treat us by the way we treat ourselves.

Because you are reading this book, I know that you are committed to your success and your pursuit of a radiant, impactful life. I know you usually stay true to your word and follow through on your personal commitments. However, we are all human, and if you have any people-pleasing tendencies, you probably have an easier time keeping the promises you make to others than the ones you make to yourself. Perhaps you justify this to yourself by thinking, *I love helping people, and the fact I am willing to do so at the expense of my own personal goals and desires just shows how unselfish I am.* But such an approach to life is not sustainable. Over time, resentment is almost certain to creep in. You may find yourself wondering why you aren't further along on your journey, or why you constantly feel so drained of energy.

Each time you push your own needs down, you tell your subconscious mind and the universe, "Someone else matters more than I do. This person's needs, timeline, and priorities are more important than my own." That does not feel so satisfying, does it? When you delay following through on the promises you have made to yourself (or neglect to do so altogether), you also hesitate to create new goals and aspirations. This creates a loop of discontentment, and you therefore move further away from your highest self. You create a habit of indecision, and your courage falters right when you need it the most.

Take a moment to sit with this for a moment. Have you been there before? I know I have. I have also seen countless other women become entrenched in this exact habit loop.

When we invest in making decisions for our highest self to flourish, and then follow through on those decisions with inspired action, our confidence, trust, and energy levels soar. We see that what we desire is achievable, and we become excited to keep showing up for ourselves. We stop relying on others to cheer us on and we become our own number one supporter and advocate. We tune into our future selves' wisdom with such precision that it feels like we can see the outcomes of the decisions we make. And yes, you can still be a compassionate and generous human being while keeping your promises to yourself. I initially thought it was selfish to put myself first, but then I trusted the process and began receiving messages from friends, co-workers, clients, and retreat participants saying that because they saw me being true to myself, they had become inspired to be more thoughtful toward themselves. Me keeping myself as a priority was not only unselfish, but one of the ways in which I helped others the most!

When I set out to make this shift in my life, I began by reading books, just as you are now. Then, I realized that I needed extra support as new mindsets and habits are not easy to keep up with alone. There are areas in life and business in which I find incredible value in having a coach to help show me a new path that I may not have considered before, or to lift me to the next level of growth which would take much more time to do on my own. One such mentor of mine, Larisa Petrini (an age reversal expert and brilliant mindset coach), could see exactly where I had been struggling as soon as we started working together several years ago. Spoiler alert: it involved me not following through on my promises to myself.

Ever since high school, I have been working on personal development. I had big hopes and dreams for myself and an insatiable desire to have a positive impact on the world. I wanted to stop family cycles of abuse and dependency and had done so much healing so I could achieve these goals. Yet I felt like I kept hitting a limit.

Larisa's insights cut through the haze of my frustration. She was able to pinpoint a profound issue that had been keeping me stuck: my low self-worth from childhood and my failure to keep promises to myself. Neither of these things were a quick fix.

The first seven years of our lives are pivotal in shaping the foundations of our beliefs, self-image, and feelings of worthiness. This period, often referred to as "early childhood" or the "critical period", is marked by rapid cognitive, emotional, and social development, and usually, it is during these years that we develop the "blocks" that make it harder for us to fulfill self-promises in adulthood. Here is a closer look at why:

- Formation of core beliefs. During this period, a child is like a sponge, absorbing information from their environment without the filters that develop later in life. Core beliefs about self-worth, love, safety, and belonging are imprinted during this stage based on the child's experiences, interactions with caregivers, and surrounding environment. Positive experiences can foster a sense of security and self-worth, while negative experiences (even just a few, whether at home, at school, or in another setting) may lead to the internalization of feelings of inadequacy.
- Neurological development. The brain undergoes rapid growth and development during these early years, with a surge in synapse formation and neural connections. This neurological plasticity makes children highly receptive to external influences, shaping their emotional responses and cognitive patterns (which become less malleable as we move into adulthood).
- Attachment and emotional bonding. The quality of the attachments formed with primary caregivers during the first seven years of life profoundly influences the child's emotional wellbeing and feelings of worthiness. Secure attachments to a positive and safe caregiver contribute to a sense of safety and trust, fostering a positive self-image, while insecure attachments can lead to difficulties in forming healthy relationships and feelings of unworthiness that persist well into adulthood. Prolonged time with non-primary caregivers (such as frequent changes in childcare or extended periods of time without the primary caregiver) can also impact secure attachment.
- Language and communication skills. During this period, language acquisition is not just about verbal communication. It also includes understanding nonverbal cues and emotional expressions. The way caregivers communicate approval, love, or disapproval significantly impacts a child's self-perception and beliefs about their worthiness.

- Modeling behavior. Children learn through observation and imitation, absorbing the behaviors and attitudes exhibited by the adults who are closest to them. Positive modeling contributes to the development of healthy self-esteem, while negative modeling can reinforce patterns of self-doubt and unworthiness.

- Establishment of patterns and paradigms. The experiences and interactions during these early years form beliefs that can become deeply ingrained, creating an internalized script that influences decision-making, relationships, and perceptions of self-worth. These permeate throughout our lifetimes unless we make a conscious decision to change.

While this is not a parenting book, I want you to understand the profound impact that our childhoods have on our development and feelings of worthiness. Clearly, we need to make a conscious effort to repattern and reframe these cognitive experiences so that we can soar as high as we desire! After all, the limits imposed on us in childhood are not just stumbling blocks; they are gatekeepers of our own sense of self-worth. This revelation hit hard once I became aware of it. If you struggle to feel deserving, this is not a mere personal shortcoming; it is the consequence of a developmental period during which you absorbed, like a sponge, the judgments and limitations imposed upon you.

There is no need for blame in this equation, whether toward the caregivers who unknowingly perpetuated these patterns or toward yourself, for carrying them into adulthood. Most likely, everyone involved has been at the mercy of their own "womb-to-seven" conditioning. Still, acknowledging the roots of your struggles is pivotal for transformation. This does not involve dismissing the past or going back to live there, but understanding its influence on the current you, so you can consciously choose a different path. In doing so, you do not just liberate yourself, but you also become an architect building a different future. By rewriting your narrative, you break the chains that bind you and of those who will follow in your footsteps. In this way, self-love, empowerment, and boundless potential become not just aspirations, but fundamental pieces to your personal legend story.

This work is not a one-time fix. It is a continuous journey. If that sounds like a lot of work, that's because it is, but it is also a lot of work to stay stuck in old stories and habits. Since both are hard, you may as well pick the "hard" that has the best outcome, right?

Assuming you have decided to do the work, let's proceed. Specifically, while we are still fairly close to the beginning of our journey together, let's put some self-promises in place.

I like to make these promises specific but open-ended. Sometimes, being overly specific doesn't allow room for magic and the natural ebbs and flows of life. An uber-specific goal like, "I will make two hundred thousand dollars by April fifteenth through my business and passive income," is a very "masculine energy" approach that can leave many women feeling defeated when the exact outcome does not happen. Do feel free to play with this structure, should it call to you, but try not to become overly attached to its outcomes. For now, I would more strongly encourage you to lean into self-promises that are aligned with the feminine frequencies to create more balance.

Here are several promises I wrote to myself earlier this year, for some inspiration. I would love to hear what your self-promises are!

I promise that I will not give up. The business I am creating and elevating is world class. It inspires others, brings me joy, and provides greater financial abundance than I could ever have imagined for myself, my family, my team, and my community.

I promise that I will nurture my body and physical wellbeing. I will treat it with the care and love of a Goddess. I will feed my divine temple with food that provides energy and health. I will move my body with ease and gentleness, strengthening muscles and increasing my flexibility and heart health.

I promise that I will take care of my mental wellbeing. I will ask for help when I need it. I will treat myself with gentleness and compassion. I will not allow emotions to control me or consume me. I will make decisions from the perspective of my highest self.

I promise to nurture my spiritual health, taking time to reconnect with my divine spirit, enjoy the daily mundane tasks of life, and fully embrace new adventures and opportunities.

I promise to make my happiness a priority; to love myself deeply and completely; to shine and to never give up on myself and my dreams!

Did any of these resonate with you?

You may be wondering why some pieces of my life are missing here. For example, my family is not mentioned at all. Here is why: I always, always, always prioritize my family. My children come first. This is a given that I never have to think about or justify to myself or to anyone else. In my mind, it is automatically a non-negotiable. It is already integrated so deeply in my life that there is never a question about whether my family is a priority. I therefore tend to keep my promise statements focused on the areas of my life which I have been apt to let slide. For example, I have previously chosen not to launch a new program for my business because I gave in to doubts about whether I was ready. This meant I delayed income for myself and my family. As another example, I have previously stayed up too late eating ice cream, and therefore not treated my body like the sacred temple it is. There have also been many times in my life where I did not ask for help when I needed it and then found myself in overwhelming situations. There have also been quite a few times where I have I neglected my spiritual health because I had been hurt by people who claimed to be my spiritual family.

Sometimes, the promises we need to make to ourselves concern the areas of our lives we have not been dedicating ourselves to. By claiming these in the form of a self-promise, our attitude changes from one of scarcity to one where we open up to abundant possibilities and make them a reality.

We begin to see so many beautiful ways in which we can create the bliss we desire and even challenge ourselves to raise the bar higher.

"When you stop living your life by other people's rules, you stop living by their beliefs, and you start living in alignment with your own soul's purpose." This message from Vishen Lakhiani, author, and founder of MindValley, stirs passion in my heart. This is the ultimate self-promise. When you begin to live in accordance with your own soul's purpose, the universe truly begins to conspire in your favor.

Goddess Inspiration: Pele (Radical Transformation)

In the vibrant traditions of Hawai'ian mythology, the goddess Pele reigns as the fiery embodiment of the volcano, passion, and the transformative power of nature. She embodies both destructive and creative forces, as well as radical transformation through overcoming obstacles. Her energy is a relentless force of creation and destruction, reminding us that transformation often requires the willingness to let go of the old and embrace the new. This is an essential part of the healing process. Just as Pele constructs new landscapes through her volcanic eruptions, she invites you to release what no longer serves you, so you can create something fresh and new that aligns with your current needs and desires that awakens your true potential. She teaches us that change is an inherent part of life and that embracing it with courage and openness can lead to tremendous growth and empowerment.

Radical transformation often requires embracing the unknown. Mapping out the support system that can accompany you on your transformative journey is therefore essential when you are making big shifts, whether those changes are external (such as a moving to another country that aligns with your values and desired lifestyle) or internal (such as allowing yourself to let go of false beliefs that do not support your future self).

To demonstrate Pele's essence, let me introduce you to Lina. She knew from a very young age that she was intuitive and could even heal others. However, as she grew older, she began to doubt her abilities. So, rather than offering her holistic services to those in need, she felt that it was "safer" to go the mainstream science route and became a pharmacy tech. While she appreciated the financial stability this role brought, she felt her career was literally eating away at her soul. Daily, customers would come to her with illnesses and symptoms that she knew could be taken care of without the harmful side effects of prescription medication. She also knew the roots of her customers' issues were not being addressed through the medicine she would dispense. It was simply "pay now, pop this pill, and return next month".

Lina was so overwhelmed, not by the responsibilities of the job (she could go through the motions on autopilot), but because she was burning out due to the emotional load that came with her not being able to express her soul gift of true healing. She felt morally misaligned with what was expected of her at work. It felt like spiritual violence. At her wits' end, she decided to go on a retreat to Hawai'i, where she was introduced to the energy of the goddess Pele. Instantly, Lina was drawn to Pele's passion and power. Legend has it that Pele created the magnificent islands of Hawai'i through her seemingly violent volcanic eruptions, and this made Lina wonder if maybe being angry about her current situation was necessary. She had been trying so hard to keep the peace in her inner world and workplace that she had begun bottling up her rage. The truth was, she was furious with the pharmaceutical industry for taking advantage of people in the name of profit. Mostly, though, she was angry with herself, for not listening to her heart for so long. She had allowed herself to be pulled away from her inner wisdom and natural healing abilities, and for what? So she could tell her parents that she had a steady income? So she could not get questioning looks from strangers when she told them she could facilitate healing naturally?

When Lina went back home to Ohio, she made a promise to herself. She wrote a mission statement for her life that included honoring her innate gifts and never letting fear dictate her life choices again.

Lina went on to secure an office space at a wellness center, where she shared her healing with clients. Her clients were eternally grateful to have access to the healing support Lina offered. Shortly thereafter, Lina put her notice of resignation in at the pharmacy, and she has never looked back since!

Just like Pele and Lina, you, too, are a vessel of transformation and empowerment. By embodying Pele's energy and keeping your self-promises, you will discover the fiery spirit within you and blaze a new trail.

Inspired Action

It is your turn! Write several promises to yourself. Take some time to tune into what really matters to you. Also consider what you have been delaying or putting on the backburner that you truly do want to pay more attention to.

I would love to hear what your promises are. Share them with me via email at hello@goddessoflightretreats.com!

3

Amplify

5

BECOME THE WOMAN OF YOUR DREAMS

———

If you're always trying to be normal, you will never know how amazing you can be.

—Maya Angelou

NOW THAT YOU HAVE YOUR SELF-PROMISES in place, it is time to truly embody the woman who lives out these promises. It is time to step into your Goddess energy.

In the pursuit of success, you may find yourself looking outward, seeking to become someone else. You may envy influencers on social media whose camera-ready hair is lust-worthy, or your co-worker who seems to have it all together while you are just trying to survive the next moment. But true success is not about becoming someone else. It is about becoming the woman *you* are meant to be. As Maya Angelou so beautifully stated, it is about embracing your true self and stepping into the power of your own amazing and unique journey.

Did you realize that everything and everyone who is in your life today, from the career you have and your partner (if you have one), to the home you live in and the clothes on your back, came into your life directly because of decisions you made in the past? This means that if you long to create a business, uplevel your health, start a new career, or attract abundance from any realm into your life, it all begins with you shifting your identity to become the woman you desire to be (and not solely relying on a previous version of yourself). Every aspect of your life is determined by your identity. It shapes your reality. If you think you are someone who magnetizes wealth and prosperity, you will show up in a way that does exactly that. If you believe that you are someone who will never have genuine, trustworthy friends, then unfortunately, you will keep attracting toxic relationships or pushing people away.

When you create goals and visions, you can only go as far as the limits of your personal identity. This means that if there is anything in your life that you are not currently one hundred percent satisfied with, some aspect of your identity will need to shift if you are to become the woman who claims and achieves those goals. To create the reality you truly desire, you must align your present actions with your vision of your *future* self. You must act, think, and speak from the place of the woman who already lives the life of her dreams and allow her to exist here in the present moment.

Consider what lights you up. Explore from within. What are you passionate about? How can you bring your passion into the work you are doing? A slight shift can have a profound impact, and if you do not bring your light forward, you will continue to live according to the woman of your past—with the same outcomes of the past—rather than the life of your dreams.

My client Elaine came to me years ago after she had made a later-in-life transition from a high-paying job in the private sector to a job pursuing her passion as a computer science and robotics teacher. She had been expecting things to fall into place after she made this decision, but things did not turn out to be that simple. She began experiencing burnout in her role as a high school teacher, even though she enjoyed her time teaching students and making a positive difference. Elaine expressed to me where she wanted to be. She wanted to spend more time with her husband, to tend to her physical and mental wellbeing, to attend regular yoga classes, and to be the teacher who advocates for inclusion and emotional wellbeing in schools.

The first thing I always do with a new client is have them explore what they can take off their plate (remember what we said about decreasing demand and increasing capacity). Everyone gets into the habit of spending time on things that do not truly make an impact or align with their higher self, so when you are looking to go through an internal transformation, it is always a great idea to start by realigning your time and energy.

Since working with me, Elaine has made significant breakthroughs. She has more tools to reduce burnout and overwhelm, she has officially founded a nonprofit organization, and she has received a top educator award. I am so proud of her for saying yes to herself by getting the support she needed, releasing what no longer served her, and taking the inspired action necessary for her to become the woman who started an organization that aligned with her values and vision. All of this happened when she took personal responsibility for her life and began to identify as the woman of her dreams and take inspired action accordingly.

Taking personal responsibility for your life means being proactive and engaged in the manifestation journey, rather than passively waiting for things to happen. By taking ownership of your deepest desires, aligning your thoughts, beliefs, and actions with your intentions, and staying committed to your goals, you actively invite the universe to conspire in your favor. How incredible is that? I see the ability to take meaningful action as an amazing gift from the universe.

When the Law of Attraction Feels Oppressive

If your childhood experience included systemic disadvantage (such as if you were born a woman of color in a segregated country, or if you experienced poverty, neglect, physical or emotional abuse, or mental illness), this may feel out of reach at times. Ideas such as the law of attraction may even feel like its own form of oppression. After all, if you are being told that you attract what you experience and you continue to face awful situations such as racism, sexism, and agism, it can feel like you are being blamed for what you have gone through. Furthermore, if you:

- Have experienced substance abuse or sexual assault/childhood molestation,
- Hold or once held religious beliefs that lie outside your country's mainstream religion,
- Do not subscribe to monogamy or heterosexuality,
- Have endured childhood bullying, and/or
- Have experienced situational, generational, or environmental trauma,

you may also have questioned if manifesting the life you truly desire deep in your soul is possible, given the conditions of your external surroundings or cultural norms.

I understand that you may have encountered times when taking action did not reap positive results, or even led to further issues. I understand that certain individuals or systems might have pushed back when you tried to manifest your dreams. I may be compassionate and optimistic, but I am also very aware that some have privileges that others do not. Even still, you *can* create meaningful change in your life and achieve your highest visions. Once you make the decision to embody your higher self, this will be noticed by everyone around you, creating ripple effects. Look for support, look for signs, and look for ways to challenge the status quo, one step at a time.

The Shift to Goddess Energy

At the end of a Goddess Retreat, we hold a closing ceremony, in which each woman takes turns honoring the other women in the circle. During one particular closing ceremony, one of the beautiful participants, Frances, said to me, "I believe that you have always known that you are a Goddess. I'm not sure how to find that within myself, but I want to learn." I was in shock at these words. To see myself through her eyes, as someone who knew her path and could light a way for others, almost brought me to my knees. Growing up, I had so much self-doubt and such low self-confidence and had often questioned my worthiness. When she said this to me, I knew that the intentional work I had done over the last two decades to become the woman that I desired to be had worked (although it is an ongoing journey!). I did not realize how much my self-worth had grown over the years until that moment.

What is incredible about this woman is that she kept attending the retreats until she realized that she, too, was worthy of reclaiming her Goddess energy. She even went on to study sound healing, so she could uplift more women and help them regain inner peace. Her intention of changing her inner world created the momentum she needed to learn how to realign her thoughts, energy, and frequency. I am forever grateful for the fact that she spoke her truth in that moment. That conversation confirmed the fact that we can change our paths and co-create the lives we desire by shifting the way we show up in the world.

Tuning Into Inspiration

On a similar note, do you recall the movie *From Homeless to Harvard*? Liz Murray, whose parents are drug addicts, finds herself homeless at fifteen years old. The storyline follows Liz through completing high school, succeeding against the odds, and entering Harvard on a scholarship in her freshman year.

I was already in college when the movie was released, and I had also beaten great odds. I was homeless for a short time in elementary school, I lived with domestic violence and parental mental illness for the first decade of my life, and I endured sexual assault weeks after my sixteenth birthday. Liz's story greatly inspired me. To see another young woman who was statistically unlikely to suceed, rise to meet the challenge of her own inner compass helped to reignite the passion within myself to keep going and believe that anything is possible.

Research shows that taking inspired action and sharing our dreams with a trusted community of likeminded individuals increases our chances of success and reaching our aspirations. According to a study by Dr. Gail Matthews at the Dominican University of California, those who wrote down their goals and shared them with others were thirty-three percent more successful in achieving them. Dreams are important, but a dream that is not shared among trusted supporters or acted upon will forever remain trapped within the mind—and your dreams deserve to see the light of day, regardless of what barriers and traumas have previously prevented you from shining like the brilliant star that you are.

When groups of women come together to share their truths and dreams, oppressive systems begin to crack. Barriers that once felt insurmountable now seem manageable. Where there was once isolation and fear, connection and courage seep into the light. Consider when a community trauma occurs such as a natural disaster: among the pain, when people of the community come together, they rebuild a new foundation together. This is humanity at its best. Similarly, when you decide you are ready to become the woman that your dreams require you to be and your support system is on the same page as you, even the direst of situations can be transformed. First, though, you must listen to your own internal compass. This "knowing" that resides within you is the voice of your future self. It is the voice of the woman who has already achieved the life of her dreams. When you tap into this inner wisdom, you can begin to determine what inspired action is needed. For this reason, when I lead retreats, we always practice listening to our intuition.

The Goddess doesn't enter us from outside; she emerges from deep within. She is not held back by what happened in the past. She is conceived in consciousness, born in love, and nurtured by higher thinking. She is integrity and value, created and sustained by the hard work of personal growth and the discipline of a life lived actively in hope.
—Marianne Williamson

Step Into Her Shoes

We are going to play a bit of a game, if you will, to fast-track your transformation. This will help you to really step into the shoes of the ideal version of yourself and align with her energy.

First, envision the woman of your dreams—your future self. Think about the way she dresses. Is she mindful about the fabrics and colors that suit her best? Visualize the jewelry and accessories that bring a sparkle to her eyes. What is she wearing on her feet? Is her personal style glamorous or more boho chic? Does she wear power suits or long, flowy dresses? By incorporating some of the choices that align with this future self's style into your present-day wardrobe, you adopt the confident persona you aspire to embody (which runs deeper than surface-level dressing up).

Now, shift your focus to her surroundings. Envision her home. What does it look like? Is it decorated with vibrant colors, or is a more subdued, minimalist look more suited to her? Are there plants or windchimes? Does she have a dresser adorned with crystals? Take a moment to meditate on or journal about what her home looks like. Then, bring aspects of this vision to life! While major changes might be impractical all at once, consider small alterations. Rearrange furniture, add meaningful decorations, or declutter to create an environment that resonates with the emotions and memories you desire to create at home.

Next, think about the activities that fill your future self's days. What brings her joy and fulfillment? Perhaps she is involved in charity work, takes salsa classes with friends, writes poetry in the park, or prioritizes family outings. By integrating these activities into your current routine, you are not just planning your schedule; you are embodying the values and passions that define your future self.

Consider the people she surrounds herself with. Is she fostering relationships that inspire and uplift her? Has she let go of old relationships that make her feel devalued, belittled, or drained? If she values community engagement, seek ways to connect with likeminded individuals. Strengthen your existing relationships and foster new connections to align your present self with the social environment you envision.

Next, determine her mindset. Is she someone who never gives up, is determined yet allows herself to grow from her mistakes? Is she someone who makes wise choices with her money, her time, her finances, and uses her resources to uplift and inspire herself and others? Is she someone who can acknowledge the hard, then keep climbing, rest when she needs rest, ask for help before it gets too be overwhelming, and is able to see the best in herself?

Now, most importantly, how does she feel? The woman that you intend to become, does she wake up in a state of gratitude and joy? Does she feel excited for new opportunities? Is she at peace with her decisions and the way she is living? Is your future self allowing herself to feel proud of her accomplishments? Does she feel generous in her interactions with others? Identify how you most desire to step into the state of emotional beingness.

In essence, stepping into your future self's shoes involves being intentional with your choices and surroundings. It is about bringing the future into the present by embodying the qualities and lifestyle you aspire to have. Each decision, whether in fashion, your environment, your activities, your relationships, or in your mindset and emotions, becomes a step forward on your path. If you stay the same, you will achieve the same. You must change the frequency (like a dial on a radio) to be available to invite new opportunities.

What steps can you take to embody the qualities and characteristics of the woman you aspire to be? Embrace her confidence, courage, resilience, and authenticity. Let these qualities radiate from every cell of your being. Recognize that you are a force of nature capable of creating and manifesting your dreams into reality. In times of uncertainty, allow yourself to connect with the wisdom of your Goddess energy. Visualize her as the embodiment of your dreams, standing tall and radiant, having overcome all obstacles and living the life you envision. Above all, trust in the divine timing of the universe. Your dreams are not merely a figment of your imagination; they are the whispers of your soul, calling you toward a purpose-filled life. Allow yourself to listen to these whispers, with the knowledge that the universe is conspiring to bring your personal legend to fruition in the perfect way and in divine time. The world eagerly awaits the radiance and brilliance that only you can bring to it!

Dress the Part

I would like to expand on the first task I just gave you: dressing the part. I do not want the seemingly simplicity of this task to be overlooked.

"Enclothed cognition" is a term that refers to the systematic influence that clothes have on the wearer's psychological processes. This term was first introduced to me by Larissa Peterini (the age reversal expert and mindset coach I mentioned earlier). Enclothed cognition refers to when the clothing a person wears impacts their cognitive functions, including their perceptions, attitudes, and behaviors. In other words, it is when what you wear influences how others perceive you, as well as how you perceive and express yourself.

The idea of enclothed cognition was first introduced in a study titled *Enclothed Cognition* by Hajo Adam and Adam D. Galinsky, published in 2012.[1] Here, the researchers conducted experiments to explore how the symbolic meaning of clothing could affect the wearers' cognitive processes. They found that individuals who wore a white lab coat (which is traditionally associated with attentiveness and carefulness) performed better on tasks requiring focused attention compared to those who did not wear a lab coat, among other interesting details related to how we dress and our behaviors. Here are some things to consider about enclothed cognition:

- Symbolic meaning. Clothing carries symbolic meaning that can influence the wearer's mindset and behavior. For example, if you are wearing a blazer and a pencil skirt, you may feel more confident, professional, and authoritative. If you have a cocktail dress on, you

---

[1] Adam, A. & Galinsky, A. D. (2012): *Enclothed Cognition.* Journal of Experimental Social Psychology, 48(4) (p.p. 918–925).

may feel more sexy, sophisticated, and spontaneous. This also applies to the colors you wear. I once knew a woman who wore black and white every day (every single day). I understand that it was easier this way—she could pull anything out of her closet and it would match—but when the day came that she donned a bright blue shirt, it was amazing to witness how her eyes popped, how her skin tone looked healthier, and she seemed more vibrant and happier. Colors are linked to emotions, so identifying two or three colors that highlight your natural complexion and make you smile can go a long way in helping you step into the shoes of the woman you are becoming.

- Identity and self-perception. Clothing can form an essential part of your self-expression and identity, as well as your confidence and performance. Imagine yourself showing up at the gym in heels and a dress. How ready would you feel to work up a sweat? Similarly, if you want to show up to work on a project that could change your life, dressing like the woman who is bringing it to reality could be the difference between treating this dream like a ten-dollar experiment or a ten-million-dollar legacy.

- Cognitive and behavioral performance. Enclothed cognition suggests that what you wear can influence your cognitive abilities. Isn't that fascinating? Now, do not let me or anyone else tell you what to wear, for that is a very personal choice. And yes, there are very wealthy and successful people who wear sweats and ballcaps more often than they wear black tie attire. Yet those people are also more likely to dress for the occasion when it is called for. When I have an important meeting online, I know that I could technically get away with wearing slippers and pajama pants and having smelly breath, but do I? Nope (well, at least ninety percent of the time)! I dress appropriately from head to toe, brush my teeth, and clear my space, because just as much as I am there for the person on the Zoom call, I am there for myself, and I want to bring the right energy and intention to the call.

It is important to note that the effects of enclothed cognition can vary from person to person. Individual differences, cultural factors, and personal beliefs all play a role in shaping the psychological impact of clothing. Additionally, ongoing research in the field continues to explore the nuances and extent of enclothed cognition. However, there is a growing consensus in academia that what we wear impacts our day-to-day behavior and decision-making. I recommend seeing what trying out a different style does for you!

Surrounded in Support

The journey to becoming the woman of your dreams is not meant to be a smooth and effortless ride. There will be challenges, obstacles, and moments of doubt that test your resilience and determination along the way. Through all of that, I want you to hold onto the belief that it is absolutely possible for you to overcome and rise above. In those moments when the road feels treacherous and the weight of self-doubt begins to creep in, reconnect with the deep "knowing" that resides within your soul. Remind yourself of the countless women who have walked this path before you and triumphed over adversity. You, too, possess that same inherent strength and resilience. It was woven into the strands of DNA that wind together to create you. This strength is in the dust of the stars that create your essence.

Often, when we are shifting our identity to become the woman who sees our ambitions through and elevates our future selves, we feel a sense of loss for who were once were. Our family, friends, and loved ones may similarly not be so thrilled about the changes we are making. This goes back to our primal need for survival. Our unconscious brain pattern is saying, "But you did it this way for so long, and you survived! If you change, there is no guarantee of survival!" This is the only way it knows how to keep us safe. But it does not always have our best, highest interests at heart.

Goddess, you are not meant to simply get by through mere survival! You are meant to thrive, elevate, rise, and shine. Playing it safe is an ego trap that can keep you stuck. Besides, I am willing to bet that you are reading this book because you are sick and tired of feeling stuck or playing small. Therefore, I encourage you to surround yourself with a supportive tribe of likeminded women who genuinely believe in your potential. Seek out those who uplift and inspire you. Grab onto those who cheer you on even when the journey feels impossible.

I understand that not everyone currently has this level of support. Still, a support network is essential if you are going to truly elevate yourself to the level you are capable of reaching. One of the primary reasons I have been able to make such significant progress in my personal and professional life is that I have intentionally sought support, mentorship, and community. When I create retreats, online memberships, and women's circles, the priority is to make the spaces safe for women to express not only their celebrations and dreams, but also their concerns and fears; to ensure everyone feels included, welcome, supported, and capable of what their heart and highest self truly desires.

Some of the feedback I most love hearing from women who have participated in my retreats, circles, or programs is that these spaces feel like a safe and cozy cocoon. These women report that once they emerge from this safe haven, they feel ready to come out and test their wings. One such woman who attended a Goddess Healing Retreat was in tears by the end of the day. She proclaimed, "I met likeminded and amazing women that I didn't know were out there. I pushed through fears of being vulnerable with strangers and allowed myself to experience new and raw beauty. It was the greatest thing I've ever done in my life!"

Another woman who attended a destination retreat in Sedona initially had some hesitations about leaving her son for several days. She was also self-conscious of the fact that she would be the youngest woman at this particular retreat. But she pushed through these worries, and from the very first day, she connected with the women who had adult children and asked for their wisdom in navigating the turbulent times that can come with parenthood. Very quickly, she felt so understood and supported by them. Commenting on her time with us, she said, "There was so much time for self-care, self-discovery, self-reflection, spiritual exploration, and sisterhood. You just need to show up and enjoy the ride!"

This type of feedback is not limited to in-person experiences. Robin M., who participated in an online coaching group I led, said, "I would absolutely recommend Marie to any professional that is making any transition or trying to re-engage with their passion. Since I've been working with Marie, I have made so many breakthroughs in my career and business, and I'm excited about it!"

Consider what support systems you currently have in place. Are you surrounding yourself with people who are encouraging you? People who are also taking inspired action? Who are working toward their highest selves? If not, what opportunities to join a community that will keep you focused on reaching your "highest self" goals do you have at your disposal? Go look for them! Be sure to be discerning, though. I have seen spaces in which the leader or creator does not hold the intention of emotional safety, or is not skilled at understanding how to hold the space for the wellbeing of those involved. It is essential for a facilitator to invest time in their own personal growth journey and to ensure that they have the training needed to navigate the challenges that may arise before they create a sacred space. While self-healing may be a great byproduct of creating retreats and circles, those bringing circles and communities together should never use the space primarily for their own benefit. They need a clear and open energy field to be able to lovingly and safely hold space for those that they serve.

Goddess Inspiration: Freyja (Fearless Freedom)

Freyja is a warrior goddess in Norse mythology symbolizing independence, strength, and fierce femininity. Her fearless spirit can help you to stand taller as you navigate your journey to your highest self. I, for one, needed

Freyja's strength as I navigated a difficult and emotionally painful career decision not long ago.

After I had my second child, it pained me to go to work each morning. I would watch my little one calling out to me as I drove away to (ironically) help other children as a school counselor. Quickly, I reached the end of my rope. It was time for me to explore ways in which I could work from home or create a different work structure so that I did not continue to miss out on all his precious moments.

I was always entrepreneurial at heart and had even been a team leader in a few MLMs. However, I would always get frustrated at how little power the reps had. I wanted to have my own business. So, I decided to begin my own coaching and consulting business, Compassionate Educators, in 2018. Through ups and downs (including the pandemic), I learned how to create a business, help others to launch their own coaching businesses, start a podcast, do tons of online networking, and develop so many other skills that lit a new passion in me. However, a few years later, I realized I had a deep desire to help local students feel safe and regulated enough to enjoy school, so, in 2022, I stepped back into an elementary school, thinking I would save the world (or at least a few students). Instead, I became physically ill. I believe this is because I was not being true to my soul's calling of creating a legacy business. Instead, I geared my efforts toward changing a system that was out of alignment, and this manifested as dis-ease. One Friday in February, while sitting in a work meeting, I felt a pain in my abdomen so severe that my general practitioner immediately urged me to go the emergency room. After weeks of tests, including an endoscopy on Valentine's Day, the results were in: the stress of the job was too much. My doctor urged me to leave.

I felt like a failure. Here I was, supporting other educators on how to reduce burnout, practice radical self-compassion, and make time for self-care, yet I was so burnt out in this experience that I could barely function. How had this happened? I had been a social worker and school counselor forever, even serving as a volunteer at a runaway shelter while I was still in high school and had always managed to find balance. My invincibility had run its course, it seemed. I needed to breathe into the energy of Freyja to summon strength.

Making the decision to leave a school community of students and staff that I had quickly grown to care deeply about felt nearly impossible. Yet I am the only one who I must answer to for the rest of my life. I have no choice but to prioritize my wellbeing and health above all else. Clearly, it was necessary for me to courageously reclaim my power, no matter how difficult or daunting this felt, and I am glad I did. After this wakeup call, I did so much more healing, realigned my business, expanded my retreats, and wrote this beautiful book (so we could connect!). I would not have been able to do any of this without Freyja's energy in my corner, and my ability to listen to and align with my future self—the one who knew that there was a way to elevate above the noise of the ego.

Inspired Action

What change do you need to create in your life to become the woman of your dreams? Does it require a courageous step forward?

I have found that one of the fastest and most powerful ways to take bold leaps is to have a guide that can help keep you pointed in the right direction, lend an ear, provide resources to help with the journey, and be an ally when life throws curveballs. This in mind, consider finding a mentor, guide, or coach that can help you connect deeper to your inner Goddess and guide you through the lens of where you are going rather than where you have been.

As a starting point, I invite you to check out ways that you and I can work together. Go to www.goddessoflightretreats.com/connect to discover exciting ways to begin!

6

THE POWER OF VISUALIZATION

———

To bring anything into your life, imagine that it's already there.
—Richard Bach

ONE WAY TO EFFECTIVELY HARNESS YOUR intuition so you can achieve your goals is through visualization. One of many people who can advocate for this is Serena Williams.

From a young age, Serena displayed a natural talent and love for tennis. Growing up in Compton, California, she faced numerous challenges and obstacles along her path to becoming a tennis champion, but Serena's unwavering determination and belief in the power of visualization propelled her forward, until she became one of the greatest athletes of all time.

Serena understood that winning matches started long before she stepped onto the court, and that the mind was just as important as physical prowess. Embracing this insight, she incorporated visualization into her training routine. In the quiet moments before practice or competition, Serena would close her eyes and transport herself into a world of vivid imagery. She would envision herself stepping onto the tennis court, feeling the familiar grip of the racket in her hand, and experiencing the flow of the smoothness of her movements as she executed each stroke with precision.

With her eyes shut, Serena could hear the cheers of the crowd as she glided across the court, her movements effortless and fluid, as if she were dancing with the tennis ball. She visualized herself serving powerful aces, returning impossible shots, and executing flawless volleys, and finally, she imagined the triumphant roars, joyous celebrations, and feeling of accomplishment that would come with her victory.

Through the power of visualization, Serena tapped into her innate ability to perform at her peak. Every detail, every movement, every triumph, was etched in her mind with such clarity and intensity before she even walked onto the pitch.

As Serena continued to refine her visualization practice, she noticed a profound shift in her performance. She began to trust her instincts, relying on her mind's eye to guide her actions. Visualization allowed Serena to anticipate her opponents' moves, react with lightning speed, and make split-second decisions on the court. It also fortified her mental resilience. In moments of pressure or adversity, Serena could draw upon the inner strength she had cultivated through visualization. She no longer saw herself as just a tennis player, but as a force to be reckoned with. She knew she was a champion capable of achieving greatness. Her visualizations became the blueprint for her success.

As Serena stepped onto the world stage, her visualizations transformed into reality. With a record-breaking number of Grand Slam titles and Olympic gold medals and an unrivaled dominance on the tennis court, Serena's story inspired (and continues to inspire) generations of aspiring athletes. She has shown them that success is not merely a result of physical aptitude, but also a product of unwavering belief, mental fortitude, and the power of visualization. Through her dedication to visualization (among other practices, of course), she harnessed her inner potential, shattered barriers, and left an indelible mark on the world of tennis.

We may not all aspire to be an all-star athlete like Serena Williams, but this incredible tool can be harnessed for any goal we have, no matter how big or small. Whether it is starting a business, writing a book, finding love, becoming the go-to expert in our field, or creating a harmonious home, visualization empowers us to step into the vision of our desires so that they can manifest into reality.

But what is visualization, exactly?

Visualization is to vividly imagine the details, sensations, and emotions associated with your aspirations. This fosters a deep sense of belief and clarity that makes it easier for you to bridge the gap between where you are now and where you want to be. So, whether you strive to be on a TEDx stage, to world school your children, or to simply make new friends, I encourage you to play with the tool of visualization so you can unlock the treasures that lie within you. A world where your dreams take shape and become your reality lies at your feet.

This is not to say that visualization is the *only* ingredient for self-actualization. Just today, I rediscovered a live video I made some years back titled "It Has Nothing to Do with Luck." In the video, I speak about the countless people who want all the "stuff"—cars, houses, vacations, degrees, and life partners—but who do not take any action to bring those desires into their lives. Maybe they dream about, wish for, and even visualize their success in great detail, but it ends there, and they fall into victimhood when it does not happen. Let's not do that in any area of our lives! Inspired action is a key ingredient that is missing for many who practice the law of attraction (and are only attracting disappointment). The reverse is also true, though: take inspired action without a clearly visualized outcome in mind, and you are unlikely to reap the rewards you seek. When you engage in energy work and visualization first, you save time, money, and energy when you are ready to take action.

Some of the benefits and successes experienced through visualization are:

- Clarity and focus. Visualization helps us gain clarity about our desires and aspirations. By visualizing the life we want to create for ourselves, we can define our goals with more precision and create a clear plan to achieve them.
- Goal achievement. Through visualization, we envision our dreams as if they have already come true. This process helps us to align our

thoughts, beliefs, and actions with our desired outcomes. This makes it easier for us to take the necessary steps to achieve our unique personal legend.

- Building confidence. By vividly imagining ourselves succeeding and achieving our dreams, we develop a deep sense of positive self-belief. This confidence propels us forward, encouraging us to take risks and overcome challenges along the way.

- Overcoming obstacles. Even Serena Williams faced numerous challenges and setbacks throughout her career, and visualization helped her to stay resilient and to overcome obstacles. By visualizing yourself finding solutions, staying focused, and persevering through difficult times, you maintain a more positive mindset and find creative ways to jump across hurdles.

- Manifestation and abundance. Countless people that are "successful" by any standards firmly believe in the power of manifesting one's desires through visualization, and attribute much success and abundance to their abilities to visualize and attract positive outcomes into their life. By consistently visualizing your goals, you, too, align your energy and intentions with the opportunities that come your way—opportunities you may not have even noticed otherwise.

Visualization Myths

Still not convinced of the power of visualization? I get it. There are a lot of misconceptions about visualization out there that would turn the most spiritually inclined person off from the idea. Let's debunk those now, so you can see why I believe visualization to be such a powerful and necessary tool.

- "If I practice visualization, I will achieve my goals. No further action needed." Reality: Visualization is a compass pointing you in the right direction, not a magic wand that instantly grants wishes. The power of visualization lies in the fact that it sparks your motivation and brings clarity to your path, not in that it does the work for you. If you don't also take inspired action, you may get stuck in Dreamland.

- "Visualization guarantees success." Reality: While visualization has the extraordinary ability to boost your performance and attract positive energy, it is not a guarantee of overnight success. Your success story is also composed of dedication, skills, knowledge, and perseverance. Think of visualization like a big, heaping spoonful of protein powder and collagen in your smoothie: it makes for an ultra-potent drink, but it is not going to give you bulging muscles all on its own! You need a focused exercise regimen for that.

- "Visualization replaces planning and strategy." Reality: Not quite, although you can plan and strategize much more effectively when you have a solid visualization practice in place. Visualization is like the song you play to get yourself ready for a hot date. It is not going to make someone fall in love with you, but it may give you the energy you need to get in the mood. Even if visualization is eighty percent of the magic, all your effort will fall short of your goal if you do not add the twenty percent of the magic that lies in strategy and action. Visualization *primes* you for success. It is not typically the success itself.

- "Visualization leads to instant results." Reality: Visualization sets your sails in the right direction, but it is your consistent effort and perseverance that will get you making waves. Trust in the process, and the rewards, dear Goddess, will be magnificent! Remember to surround yourself with people who are also on the path of pursuing their dreams to keep your motivation high when challenges arise.

- "Visualization is only about imagining the end result." Reality: I invite you to envision not only the destination, but also the exhilarating journey that will lead you there. Visualize each step. Visualize the obstacles you may encounter and how you will move past them. Visualize the people who will be present to support you.

Visualize the small wins along the way. All of this will really set you up for a divine experience.

- "Visualization is a one-time activity." Reality: Sorry, but absolutely not! Visualization is your ongoing rendezvous with the extraordinary. This would be like saying you only need to brush your teeth once in your life. Yikes! Embrace your visualization practice as a sacred ritual that fuels your spirit daily. Add it to your calendar or tack it onto an existing habit until it becomes second nature.

- "Visualization is only for athletes or performers." Reality: If you want to be a master at creating the life you desire, visualization is a gamechanger, whether you are exploring visionary business strategies, embracing new ways of peaceful parenting, or looking for your soulmate.

- "Visualization is just wishful thinking." Reality: Oh, but it is so much more! Visualization is the portal through which you manifest your desires. Once you become crystal clear about your path and can see it, taste it, and touch it, small shifts begin to happen that lead to what you envision. With each visualization, you build an unshakable belief in your potential, and you co-create the frequencies and opportunities that bring your deepest desires into physical form.

The Science of Visualization

Still not convinced? No problem. Let's look at what the science has to say about visualization.

Extensive research on visualization supports the profound impact of visualization on our mindset, behavior, and overall success. For example, research conducted by psychologist Dr. Alan Richardson demonstrated that athletes who incorporated visualization techniques into their training routines (such as in the Serena Willaims example we explored before) showcased measurable improvements in performance compared with those who relied solely on physical practice. Furthermore, research has found that individuals who engaged in regular visualization experienced a significant decrease in stress levels and improvement in mental and physical health. The power of visualization in this regard lies in its ability to activate the relaxation response, calming the nervous system and promoting a sense of inner harmony and balance. Moreover, as renowned psychologist and author Dr. Denis Waitley explains, visualization creates a "mental blueprint" that aligns our thoughts, feelings, and actions with our desired outcomes, increasing the likelihood of success. Author and speaker Shannon Kaiser beautifully describes visualization as "a powerful tool that allows us to paint our dreams into existence. When we see it clearly in our minds, we can hold it in our hands."

The findings speak for themselves. By vividly imagining the achievement of our goals, we activate neural pathways, enhance performance, reduce stress, boost motivation, and align our energy with the outcomes we seek.

Putting Visualization into Practice

To visualize your goals effectively, it is important for you to use as many of your senses as possible. This means not just *seeing* the images in your mind, but also *feeling* the emotions and bodily sensations associated with you achieving that goal. For example, if your goal is to run a marathon, then you need to feel the impact of your soles on the pavement, the wind blowing wisps of hair off your face, your lungs moving oxygen effortlessly throughout your body, and a solid feeling of determination in your gut. You need to see, hear, smell, and feel what it would be like to cross the finish line feeling strong, confident, and energized, with a big, radiant smile on your face.

I love releasing an intention for myself into the universe, visualizing the beauty and joy it holds, and saying (in the words of Shakti Gawain), "This or something better now manifests for me in totally satisfying and harmonious ways, for the highest good for all concerned." With this statement, I release any attachment to emotions of shame, guilt, or restriction, because the intention is for the highest good of all, not just me. This generosity of spirit supports my ability to visualize and manifest miracles without restriction.

As another idea, renowned actor and comedian Jim Carrey is known for writing himself a check for ten million dollars for "acting services rendered" long before he became successful. For years, he carried this check around and visualized himself receiving such a payment. Eventually, he landed a role that earned him exactly that amount.

Jim got creative with his visualization technique, and you can, too. The more playfulness you can embody during your visualization practice, the better. Try writing a check (if you still happen to have a checkbook) or creating an invoice template with the amount of money you desire to be paid on it. Alternatively, if there is not a specific amount of money you are wanting to bring forward, get clear on what your goal is and create a tangible item that can represent how it will feel to co-create this reality. For example, if you wish to start a business, then create a business card with your services listed on it. If you are calling in the love of your life, write a love letter to your future lover. If you want to travel to a specific destination, download photos from the place your heart is longing to visit and set it as your phone's lockscreen. Make your visualization practice so juicy, delightful, and ever-present that it feels as if your visions is already being drawn to you.

Another inspiring proponent of visualization is the founder of Spanx and Shark Tank guest investor, Sara Blakely. At twenty-seven years old, Sara was selling fax machines door to door. As she did the rounds, she formed a dream. She was determined to create a pantyhose that were more comfortable for women than the traditional ones she had to wear for work. She took inspired action, made bold decisions, and took risks by investing thousands into her business before she had any physical evidence that it would lead anywhere. At the age of forty-one, Sara was celebrated as the youngest self-made female billionaire in the world and recognized as one of the most influential women on the planet. This is the power of having faith in a dream.

You can also take Beyoncé's approach. The American singer, songwriter, and actress is known for having an alter ego named Sasha Fierce. Beyoncé introduced this alter ego during the promotion of her third studio album, *I Am... Sasha Fierce*. The album was a defining moment in her career. Sasha Fierce represented a more assertive, confident, and bold side of Beyoncé's personality that she would channel during her performances. Beyoncé explained that Sasha Fierce was a stage persona, to help her overcome her natural shyness and transform her into a dynamic performer. She described Sasha as a fearless and empowered alter ego that allowed her to tap into a different energy when she was onstage, giving her the ability to take on a more commanding presence. Over the years, Beyoncé has incorporated the Sasha Fierce persona into her performances and music. She has said since then that she no longer needs the alter ego to perform with confidence: Beyoncé just *is* Sasha Fierce, and Sasha Fierce is Beyoncé. They have become one and the same.

Visualization in Everyday Life

Several years ago, I planned a retreat in southern California. I felt that going back to my birthplace of San Diego would be a beautiful way for me to honor my upcoming fortieth birthday. While researching, I learned of an enchanting spa in the area named Glen Ivy Hot Springs, and immediately knew that we needed to visit their healing mineral pools, body masque treatment, and detoxifying mud bath. It all sounded so dreamy and surreal!

Not long after I made the reservation, I found myself scrolling through a digital vision board I had created a few years prior, and I could not believe what I saw. Imagine my surprise when one of the pictures on my vision board was an *exact photo* I had just seen of Glen Ivy Hot Springs! I had not known where the photo was from when creating the vision board; I had just known that I needed this beautiful photo of the pool on my board. And there I was a few years later, enjoying every moment of the experience!

I hope these stories of what happens when people couple visualization with inspired action makes your goals feel more in reach for you as well. We all have to start somewhere, and visualization is a great way to begin.

If you are feeling held back by nerves around the prospect of stepping into the identity of your future self, consider what your alter ego's personality and energy may look, sound, and feel like. Don't worry; this is just between us! Envisioning an alternate version of yourself does not mean that you do not appreciate your own unique way of being in the world. This exercise is just a tool to support you in trying on a new version of yourself, like a new empowering wardrobe that is free and designed by you! It is possible to be grateful for your current reality *and* to consider and model your future self's thoughts, support circle, way of thinking, and daily actions. By doing so, you give yourself the opportunity to create your thoughts and to not allow old habits, patterns, and harmful generational beliefs to control you and your future.

To get started with visualization, find a quiet, comfortable space where you will not be interrupted. Close your eyes and take a few deep breaths to relax your body and mind. Then, visualize your desired outcome as vividly and in as much detail as possible. Imagine yourself achieving your goal. Feel the emotions and sensations associated with this experience. If you find it difficult to visualize, try using a vision board or other visual aids to help bring your goal to life.

If you struggle with this the first time you try it, I urge you to not give up. It is one of the foundations to creating the life you truly desire, and it gets easier and easier the more you practice.

Goddess Inspiration: Oshun (Wealth and Prosperity)

In the vibrant traditions of the Yoruba people of West Africa, the Goddess Oshun reigns as a luminous symbol of sensuality and abundance. Oshun is believed to bring success and prosperity to those who honor her. Note that the terms "abundance" and "wealth" are not limited to financial wealth (although they certainly can refer to that) and take a moment to visualize what wealth means to you. Is it an abundance of social connections, incredible health and wellbeing, or a prosperous, loving relationship? I want you to be financially healthy as well, of course, but do not stop there. Consider all the areas in your life in which you desire to be positively fulfilled.

Oshun's essence holds the key to your own abundance and prosperity. This starts with a deep sense of gratitude and appreciation for the beauty that surrounds you. Take the time to savor the sweetness of life, to indulge in the pleasures of the senses, and to immerse yourself in the joyful moments that bring you delight. By embracing the sensuality of existence, you expand the creativity and passion that resides within you. You can also visualize and feel into how your senses will respond when you have the prosperity and wealth you desire.

At my Goddess Retreats, I create space for dance. This draws the feminine flow of Oshun's abundance and sensuality forward in a natural and playful way. However, I have discovered that some women are uncomfortable with or feel awkward about dancing, especially if they are asked to move their hips or touch their bodies. They have internalized society's messaging that this is sexual, and that sexual is bad.

Sexual energy comes from the root and sacral chakra at the base of our being. These chakras are also connected to feelings of safety (the root chakra) and creativity (the sacral chakra). Therefore, opening our energy through safe sensual practices such as dancing can also help us to feel more secure in the world and to elevate our creativity. When this happens, prosperity has a clear door through which to enter our lives!

Here is an easy way to determine if you have a block at the intersection of the root and sacral chakras (such a block would prevent you from receiving all the wealth that is available to you): turn on some music (maybe some Latin music, such as salsa, as it naturally has a sensual flow), move your hips in a circle, and feel the curves of your body. What thoughts and feelings move through you as you take this inspired action? If they are fun and flowing, perfecto! You likely have a lot of freedom and space in this area. On the other hand, if you feel "stuck", this is a sign that your abundance may be blocked here.

I discovered so much freedom, joy, and self-love through dancing that I knew I needed it to be a key inclusion in my Goddess Retreats. I happened to meet Brooke Yantzi, founder of Dance Alchemy, at that time, and I shortly after became certified as a Dance Alchemy instructor. This meant I could offer more support and structure to the women I guided. Our purpose is to help people remember their truth and purpose and to help them heal through movement and dance. We guide them to a place where they can find pleasure and prosperity in movement so they can move through our lives open to receiving the abundance available in each moment. If you ever come across a practice or activity that you would love to try but do not feel quite ready to explore yet, use the power of visualization to prep yourself, even to dance!

Oshun teaches us that abundance is not solely about material wealth. It also encompasses the richness of experience, connection, and inner fulfillment. So, embrace a mindset of abundance and know that the universe is endlessly willing to provide for your needs and desires. Allow yourself to be open to the abundant flow of blessings. And when in doubt, dance it out!

Remember, if you can see it for yourself, it exists in some realm. It is just a matter of bringing it forward!

Inspired Action

Step into the magic of visualization for yourself by downloading a complementary guided visualization, available at the following link: www.goddessoflightretreats.com/visualize.

Flow

7
SACRED PORTALS OF TRANSFORMATION

——

A circle of women may just be the most powerful force known to humanity.
If you have one, embrace it. If you need one, seek it. If you find one, for the
love of all that is good and holy, dive in. Hold on. Love it up. Get naked. Let
them see you. Let them hold you. Let your reluctant tears fall. Let yourself
rise fierce and love gentle. You will be changed. The very fabric of your being
will be altered by this, if you allow it. Please, please allow it.
—Jeanette LeBlanc

I HAVE BEEN IN LOVE WITH attending and facilitating retreats and circles for so long that they have become a part of my DNA. I consider myself incredibly fortunate to have been immersed in the retreat culture since my early twenties. The first women's-only retreat I attended had a particularly profound impact on my life and pointed the direction for the way I wanted to interact with the world.

The summer following my college graduation, I found myself in a serene Zen Buddhist community nestled near the shores of Lake Michigan. Surrounded by colorful gardens, this oasis of tranquility quickly became my refuge. There, I discovered the true essence of sisterhood. The community's shared commitment to mindfulness allowed every one of us to let go of competition, jealousy, and the constant craving for men's (and each other's) approval. Under the warm summer sun, we dove into creative practices that nurtured our souls. We did meditation sessions and created bonfires by the lake. We painted and sculpted in the shade of the DeKoven Center trees. The gentle hum of singing bowls and bumblebees in the garden formed the daily rhythm of every day. Each moment was a meditation in and of itself; an opportunity to be fully present.

Meals were a sacred ritual where the community of women gathered in gratitude. We enjoyed simple yet delicious vegetarian dishes, sharing stories from our lives and from our favorite novels and movies. The laughter flowed freely, echoing through the gardens like a joyful melody. As I immersed myself deeper in the experience, something profound happened. I began to accept myself as a unique being with my own path. I saw my own beauty reflected back at me like a mirror in the eyes of my newfound sisters.

The word *namaste* is an expression that can be interpreted as, "The light in me sees the light in you," and this is exactly what happened at these retreats. In this sanctuary, we only sought the approval of our own hearts, we supported one another's dreams and aspirations without hesitation, and we were set free from the chains of conformity. Our true selves bloomed and I learned to trust myself, and other women, healing wounds that had been etched into my heart.

As all good things must come to an end, our beloved community ultimately separated. However, I knew deep within me that I could not let the magic we had experienced fade into distant memory. The joy, the laughter, the transformation, was too precious to be forgotten. And so, with a heart longing to recreate a space where others could experience the essence of the joy and magic that had transformed my life, I began a new journey. I gathered likeminded souls who carried the ember of that communal fire within them, and together, we used our gifts, strengths, passions, and stories to create new healing circles and retreats which have been repeatedly called "lifechanging" by participants.

The Need to Retreat

While I was working full-time in a high-stress environment and raising three children, I found myself on the brink of burnout. Each day felt like a marathon as I raced from one obligation to another with no time to catch my breath. The relentless pressure was nearly unbearable, and my body started to rebel against the relentless pace.

Soon enough, physical ailments began to manifest, as if my body was screaming for me to stop and take notice. My constant fatigue and physical pains were a wakeup call I could not ignore any longer. I needed a break and to pay attention to my own needs. Thankfully, I had a Goddess Healing Retreat planned. This would be a chance for me to step away from the chaos of my everyday life, slow down, refocus, and restore.

During my retreats, we create a safe space for all the women to tap into their divine, authentic selves; to be present for themselves and for one another. We engage in nurturing practices, that may include guided meditation and gentle all-levels yoga to healing rituals and creative practices. We also connect with Mother Earth as much as possible. The space quickly becomes a refuge where vulnerability is met with compassion and the weight of our burdens is shared and lightened.

In that sacred, healing space of my Goddess Healing Retreat in the midst of my burnout, I rediscovered the power of being present and nurturing myself (even though I was the one facilitating the retreat). The constant chatter of my mind quieted, and I began to embrace the stillness within again. With each breath, I released the tension that had built up within me, allowing my body to surrender to the healing energy of the retreat.

Slowly but surely, the physical ailments that had brought me to my knees began to subside and my energy levels felt replenished. It was as if my body was finding its equilibrium again.

I reconnected with my inner strength and intuitive wisdom and remembered that my wellbeing was not a luxury but a necessity if I was to show up as my best self, both for my family and for myself.

Every retreat gives me the same hope it gives to every one of the dozens of women who attend retreat with me: a renewed sense of peace and alignment, from the inside out. Understanding the power of slowing down, refocusing, and nurturing ourselves is a start, but actually taking the action and showing up to a retreat is what truly opens the door to change. During that all-important break, I was reminded of the importance of creating moments of sacred stillness amidst the chaos.

Now, dear Goddess, I wish the same for you. I wish for you to find that sacred space within yourself where you can slow down and nurture your being. I wish for you to allow yourself the grace to prioritize self-care and create moments of peace and alignment. The space of a retreat, whether online or, preferably, in person, may be the container in which you discover you can move freely, connect to your heart, rediscover your passions, and live in a way that honors your own divinity. I would certainly say it is worth a try!

Essential Elements for a Transformational Retreat

I hear the word "retreat" used so often for events that are not, in fact, retreats. This leads to a lot of confusion about what a retreat really is. I have seen what I would call business workshops, educational summits, and group trips all be branded and labeled as retreats. Is it because the word sounds sexier than "meeting"? Let's get clearer on what a retreat must include for it to truly have the capacity for true transformation, so you know what a retreat does and does not look like to help you make a more informed decision about weaving one (or more!) into your future-self journey.

Introspection

For starters, for a gathering to qualify as a retreat, there needs to be the time and space available for introspection (introspection being the thoughtful examination of our thoughts, emotions, and life experiences). This process involves engaging in a dialogue with our own psyche, whether through peaceful reflection, journaling, meditation, or a walk in the woods, in a personal quest to understand what drives us.

Why must introspection be a key element in any retreat? Because a retreat by definition is to pull back and withdraw. Retreats are all about reconnecting with the self, and you cannot do that without introspection. Introspection forms the core of your self-awareness. It allows you to pinpoint your core values, beliefs, strengths, and perhaps even those moments you would rather forget. Through this process, you get to become your own investigator, peeling back the layers of your life story to reveal what your highest self is calling you to explore.

Introspection is not just about dwelling on the past, though. It is a potent tool for navigating your present path and sculpting your future terrain. If you have ever found yourself at a crossroads, pondering, "What's my true path here?" that is where introspection is essential, and that is where retreats can be great facilitators for that journey.

A few ways in which I offer space for introspection at my retreats include intentional journaling, visualization, reflections after practices such as reiki and sound baths, nature walks, and creative practices. Activities such as these are a key element for creating space for transformation to thrive.

I have attended several workshops labeled as "retreats" that have a keynote speaker, maybe a few activities, social time, and always a lot of teaching. During these so-called retreats, participants spend their time taking notes on what the facilitator is saying, and are given minimum time, if any, for processing and integration to happen. This type of event is very useful for teaching a new skill or methodology (particularly when participants take the initiative of reflecting on what they learned afterward), but without the introspection element *during* the event, it falls flat as a retreat.

Rituals

The second crucial component that a transformational retreat includes is ceremonies or rituals. Contrary to popular belief, these do not need to have religious elements or undertones. A ritual can be as simple as taking a moment for silent gratitude before a meal, clearing the space with intention before a gathering, or a bit more elaborate such a fire release ceremony or one of my favorite Goddess retreat rituals, the rose shower.

Rituals play a pivotal role in retreat experiences, as they provide structure, meaning, and a sense of connection between participants. The importance of rituals in a retreat setting cannot be overstated.

One of the primary reasons why rituals are so significant in a retreat is, they help participants transition from their everyday lives into a more mindful, reflective, and intentional state. In other words, they mark a clear shift from the ordinary to the extraordinary, setting the stage for a retreat's unique atmosphere. They serve as a symbolic bridge between the mundane and the sacred, allowing participants to leave behind the distractions of daily life and enter a space of heightened awareness.

Additionally, ceremonies provide a sense of community and shared experience among retreat participants. By engaging in these activities together, attendees establish a shared bond, a sense of unity, and a feeling of belonging from the word "go". This enhances the sense of connection and support they feel during and after the retreat. It is especially important to promote this when the retreat in question is focused on personal growth, healing, wellness, relationships, or self-discovery.

Several types of rituals can be incorporated into a retreat. Here are some ideas.

- Opening and closing ceremonies. These rituals mark the beginning and end of a retreat, framing the entire experience and setting a collective tone for the retreat. These ceremonies can involve lighting candles, reciting affirmations, sharing intentions, honoring ancestors, and more. As I mentioned previously, my former co-facilitator for my Goddess Healing Retreats, Lesa DeBergh (who is now an angel in the spiritual realm), introduced me to a beautiful ritual that we now use as our closing ceremony: a rose shower ceremony. This is a beautiful moment when each woman showers blessings onto another, practices receiving blessings from the other women, and reflects on the transformations and connections they went through during their time at the retreat. I was honored to lead a rose ceremony for my Lesa just days before she passed in hospice. Two previous retreat participants and her son joined me, and it was a truly sacred moment. The final time I witnessed her eyes light up was when she saw her son showering her with rose petals and blessings. I still do this ceremony at my retreats to this day, and will continue to do so in her honor. It is a wonderful way to celebrate each woman as an awakened Goddess and to send love and gratitude to Lesa for all of the roles she played in my life (and in the creation of the retreats). This is the power of ceremony.

- Meditation and mindfulness rituals. Guided meditation sessions, mindful walking, and silent contemplation can be used as rituals in a retreat. These practices encourage participants to stay present and cultivate inner peace. Revisit Chapter 2 to explore this point more and to learn why it is essential to bring mindfulness activities into a space that elevates the mind, body, and soul. This is another opportunity to help participants bring deeper reflection and introspection to the retreat.

- Nature-based rituals. Retreats held in natural settings should incorporate rituals that honor the environment, though they can technically be done anywhere. These could be gratitude ceremonies or rituals involving elements like water, fire, or earth. We can bless the water, earth, air, fire, plants, and animals whether we are in retreat in the middle of a nature preserve or in the center of a city. Either way, these rituals offer a perfect opportunity to be present with the interconnectedness of all elements and sentient beings.

- Healing and cleansing rituals. Retreats focused on emotional or physical healing may incorporate rituals like sound baths or smudging (with sage or palo santo), or activities that involve releasing past traumas and limiting beliefs. This kind of ritual fits well at the beginning of a retreat, as it sets the tone for the rest of the day. If it is a multi-day retreat, it can be beneficial to include this type of ritual at the start of each day so that each morning begins anew, and the participants feel that each day is a fresh start with unlimited opportunities.

- Sharing circles. A common ritual in many retreats, sharing circles provide participants with a safe space to express themselves, share their experiences, and offer support to one another. I do encourage anyone who wants to host a sharing or reflection circle to be well-versed in trauma-informed practices and to have learned how to hold a safe space for sharing, so that participants walk away feeling supported (rather than questioning whether they should have shared their deep feelings, experiences, and insights). We feel very vulnerable when we are asked to share from our hearts, so I take this responsibility very seriously. If you need more support in hosting a circle or retreat, I offer a limited number of spots each month to support healers, coaches, therapists, wellness experts, and creatives in bringing their own retreats to life, or to make their events even more potent and meaningful. Do reach out if you would like support in this area.

- Creative expression rituals. Activities such as art, dancing, singing, and chanting encourage self-expression, creativity, and catharsis. They also bring participants closer to their passions. The fun part about creative rituals is that they can look so different based on the retreat facilitators and the participants, because everyone brings their own experiences and unique styles to the table. It can also be a time for women to release self-judgment. I recall one woman at a retreat who began the creative practice by saying, "I'm not creative!" By the end of it, she was holding a beautiful suncatcher that she crafted. She proudly displayed it for a photo and explained that the colors represented the ocean. She had claimed she was not creative, yet she had an entire story to go along with her creation!

It is moments like this that inspire me to keep sharing the magic of retreats.

- Release ceremonies. These rituals help participants to let go of what no longer serves them and to express gratitude for what they have. They often involve writing down intentions, wishes, or things you wish to release, and then symbolically burning them, burying them, or releasing them into a body of water. I personally like bringing the element of fire into this ritual, as we can watch the things we want to let go of literally go up in smoke. Burn, baby, burn! Just as a forest fire provides the necessary space and nutrients for new growth, we also need to let go and release what no longer serves us to make space for what our future selves need and desire.

By incorporating a variety of rituals into a retreat, a rich and meaningful experience is created that lingers in the hearts and minds of attendees long after the retreat has concluded. As author Terry Tempest Williams eloquently stated, "Rituals are the formula by which harmony is restored."

Retreat Myths

Retreats are a soul calling for me. However, there are some misconceptions about them that sometimes cause women who are craving a safe place to renew, heal, and connect to her highest self to shy away from saying yes to these unforgettable experiences. I want to take a moment to address them. "Retreats are solely for relaxation." Reality: While retreats do provide an opportunity for relaxation, they are not all solely focused on rest and leisure. Many retreats (my Goddess of Light Retreats included) are designed to encourage transformative experiences, personal development, skill-building, or intensive learning in a specific area. They can involve structured activities, workshops, and sessions aimed at personal or professional growth. I personally love having at least one adventurous activity at my destination retreats that take my participants out of their comfort zone, so that they can witness how courageous they truly are. Examples are kayaking, snorkeling in the Pacific Ocean, or ziplining through the jungle in Costa Rica. Not exactly relaxing, but definitely transformative!

- "Retreats always have a spiritual or religious purpose." Reality: Retreats can certainly have a spiritual or religious focus, but there are numerous retreats that cater to diverse interests and goals. Retreats can focus on wellness, mindfulness, creativity, leadership, entrepreneurship, physical activities, and many other areas of personal or professional development, from photography and writing to cooking and cultural immersion. When women join my private coaching to receive guidance and support in designing their own retreat, there are no limitations around what can be created, and there is certainly no obligation to include spiritual or religious practices, if that does not resonate. One of my mentors hosts online retreats focused on self-expression through art, while another woman I know leads retreats in France focused on wine tastings in the countryside. The options are limitless!

- "All retreats are expensive and exclusive." Reality: While my Goddess Destination Retreats include luxury experiences in different parts of the world that may include all-inclusive tours, eco-chic retreat centers, photography services, and full pampering services, I understand that some women are not yet comfortable with investing or are able to invest in themselves at that level. This is one of the reasons why I created one-day retreats that offer immense value without participants having to invest lots of time and money or travel far. Some retreats out there offer opportunities such as scholarships or work exchanges. Others are specifically designed to be budget retreats. So, for those who hear the word "retreat" and immediately think it is not doable, do some investigating into how it may be "workoutable." You never know whether it is within reach until you stretch yourself a bit!

- "Retreats are only for those seeking solitude and silence." Reality: While at the Zen center, I participated in and co-led several silent retreats. This is not typical. Retreats *can* offer a chance for solitude and self-reflection, but group retreats often provide opportunities for networking, collaboration, and relationship building. I love when women can create together, laugh together, play together, and connect in new ways that are not possible when there is only silence and solitude. The message that I always receive from my future self when designing the structure of a retreat is "balance", so my retreats are never fully focused on only solitude or only socialization; there is always a mix, and room for both.

- "Retreats require a significant time commitment." Reality: While some retreats may span several days or even weeks, not all retreats require a significant time investment. There are one-day or weekend retreats that are designed to be accessible to individuals with time constraints. Whether you are running a business, are caring for children or elderly parents, or have pets that you cannot leave for more than a day or two, joining a retreat is never out of reach. In fact, they can help you feel like you have *more time*, because they make you feel more clear-headed, calm, focused, and in a state of flow.

- "Only vegans or yogis attend retreats." Reality: Definitely not! There are certainly many retreats that focus on a vegan lifestyle or yoga as an activity, but this is absolutely not the case for all retreats. Personally, I am not vegan, though I do prefer plant-based meals while I am on a retreat, because I am even more intentional about where my food is sourced from while I am in a space of deep mindfulness. So far, I happen to have included yoga sessions in all the retreats I have hosted, because of the immense benefits it offers, but some women prefer retreats that do not include yoga. Find a retreat that speaks to your personal values and desired benefits and go from there.

- "Retreats guarantee instant transformation." Reality: While retreats can be transformative experiences, it is important to recognize that personal growth is a continuous journey. Retreats can provide a supportive environment, tools, and insights for long-term growth, but lasting change requires the ongoing integration of the learnings gained. With that said, I have watched countless women have breakthroughs during retreats that are so significant that they change the trajectory of their lives completely afterward. Breaking out of your comfort zone and engaging in practices that purposefully expand your awareness and confidence can create radical results. Still, they are never guaranteed in any retreat or program.

- "I need to be an extrovert to enjoy retreats." Reality: Since I am more on the introverted side, I tend to attract many women who are also somewhat introverted. The beauty of an intentional retreat is that everyone is honored and respected for exactly who they are. I have hosted plenty of women who were concerned about the fact that they would not know anyone else on the trip, and by the end, they were glowing and delighted to have made new friendships! Women who are extroverted may learn how to be more comfortable in stillness during retreat, while women who tend to need more alone time may discover that they have a knack for deep conversations with people they just met. A skilled host will never create judgement about your level of participation, but will provide space and opportunity for both comfort and growth.

Travel is not a luxury. It is a necessity for the soul.
—Marie Kueny

Your Personal Retreat

Consider for a moment what you would love to gain from a retreat. What in this chapter stood out to you? Did you receive any downloads about the kind of retreat you would like to participate in? Are there any specific locations that you have been longing to travel to, and the idea of going with a group of women who are intentional about elevating their lives feels exciting? I would love to know which locations your heart is asking for, and what types of retreats are calling to you! Send an email to hello@goddessoflightretreats.com with the subject line "Retreat Wishes" to tell me all about your retreat dreams.

In addition to my group retreats, I love to customize retreat experiences. In my VIP experiences, I host one or two women as a personal concierge and design a retreat filled with services and excursions tailored specifically to their wildest dreams. I love creating these itineraries and taking care of the details, and I always ensure these Goddesses receive a VIP retreat that aligns with who they desire their future self to be. Whether it is a day of deep energy cleansing followed by a traditional tea ceremony in Japan or a day of yoga and a camel ride by the pyramids of Egypt, all of it is possible when you remember that you are a Goddess!

Goddess Inspiration: Tara (Spiritual Connection and Service)

Within Tibetan Buddhism and Hinduism, the Goddess Tara is a figurehead of compassion and enlightenment. Tara is revered for her role as a protector and nurturer and is regarded as a *bodhisattva* (an enlightened being). In Buddhism, a *bodhisattva* is committed to compassionately guiding others toward an awakening.

As the embodiment of compassionate service, Tara represents swift and selfless action in times of distress and protection. She is committed to alleviating suffering and guiding all beings toward liberation. Her name, derived from the Sanskrit word *tar*, means "star" or "guide", emphasizes her role as a guiding light in the spiritual journey.

"Servant leader" is a common phrase in the leadership world (especially within the nonprofit sector), and so it comes to my mind when I think of being of service. However, I personally am not fond of this term. The word "servant" has very heavy historical and cultural connotations that would take a separate book to unpack. I instead like to use the phrase "being of service."

Consider how you could be of service to others. What are your passions? Your skills? The things that bring you solace or excitement?

I wanted to become a certified yoga teacher for years before I finally took the plunge. I wasted so much time buying into my ego's excuses for why I couldn't or shouldn't. "It costs too much - maybe I will be able to afford it later," I thought. Consider, are you stopping yourself from doing something you know would benefit you or others because of the fear that it won't be "worth" the investment? Time and money are the most common excuses that stand in the way of us embodying Tara's essence. I remember thinking, "I am too busy right now," and I still cannot believe I said this while I was working one job with no children. I now know that so much of my time was truly my own! Want to know when I finally signed up for my 200HR yoga teacher training? While I was in debt and caring for my third child. When I first considered jumping in years ago, time freedom and financial freedom were truly mine, but I didn't see it. My mind simply got in the way of my heart's calling. I allowed the excuses to overshadow the benefits. Finally, I decided that there would always be an external reason to not listen to my inner voice, so I had to take inspired action and just sign up once and for all. This was me stepping into my inner Tara.

What excuses might you be holding onto? What aspect of your life is not what you truly know it could be, because you are stopping yourself from listening to the wisdom of your heart?

I did not *need* to become a certified yoga teacher. I had plenty of degrees, certifications, and experience to be able to help my community in other ways. Yet I knew that I could not guide others to the degree I wanted to if I did not channel my energy into the proper training. You could say it was ultimately divine timing that pushed me over the edge. I came across a yoga training program based in Rishikesh, India, the birthplace of yoga. So, my (eventual) training was likely more authentic than anything I would have experienced, had I taken the training years ago. Yet, we can even use divine timing as an excuse to delay our inspired action. Welcoming the influence of Tara in your life will bring forth a profound sense of purpose and meaning, and, importantly, encourage you to take that leap.

Inspired Action

Consider the question I asked earlier: "What would you love to do more of? How can you share this with others?" This is where I start every time I create a retreat. If you love to garden, can you channel this passion into creating a small community garden? If you love to read, can you volunteer to tutor students at a local school? If you enjoy cooking, can you host a healthy cooking demo in your community? If you want to spend more time traveling, can you join a retreat? The opportunities to be of service in a way that helps you to connect to your personal wisdom and joy are endless.

Remember to send me an email at hello@goddessoflightretreats.com with a subject line of "Retreat Wishes" to tell me all about the retreat of your dreams!

8

EVOLVING INTO FLOW

———

Real change, enduring change, happens one step at a time.
—Ruth Bader Ginsburg

L ET'S TALK FOR A MOMENT ABOUT the phrase "quantum leap."
This term is taken from the principles of quantum mechanics, the branch of physics that deals with the behavior of matter and energy at the atomic and subatomic level. We will not explore this concept so much at the physics level in this book; rather, we will explore the way in which this idea is used in personal and professional growth contexts.

The quantum level is where we can jump timelines, shift reality, and choose our own paradigm. Therefore, "to quantum leap" is often used metaphorically to describe a significant and abrupt advancement, breakthrough, or change. It suggests a leap forward that is so significant that it may appear to defy conventional expectations of progress. It is a momentous and often-unexpected shift from one state or level to another, typically in a positive and transformative way. "Quantum leaping" can happen in any area of life that you want to make changes to or expand in really beautiful ways.

Within the last few years, you may have heard entrepreneurs and business owners claim that they are "quantum leaping", perhaps when they shift from having a startup business with zero profit to making six and seven figures in a short amount of time. I personally know some very financially successful entrepreneurs, and I have celebrated their "quantum leap-style" accomplishments by their side. However, I have seen that while their road to success might look glamorous from the outside looking in, each one of them has actually faced significant challenges, both internal and external, that they had to surmount in order to enter their current flow of financial abundance. I have also watched numerous CEOs, coaches, wellness experts, founders, and the like struggle with self-doubt because they do not understand why it seems that everyone else is making monumental shifts while they are just trying their hardest to stay afloat.

What many do not see is that lasting success is built one customer, one client, one course, one book, one website, one retreat, one moment at a time. Then, at some point, momentum kicks in. One person learns about a great product or service, so they tell a friend, and that friend tells two friends, and so on. This is when those "quantum leaps" happen. Unfortunately, many individuals throw in the towel right before they see this point, feeling as though they have been "left behind" or must be doing something wrong.

We may go months without seeing a friend, and then when we do, we are astonished to find that they have shed twenty pounds, or are now in love with a new partner, or have stepped into a promotion in their job and upgraded their home. In this situation, we have not been on the recent journey with that person, so it can *feel* like they have "quantum leaped." But the reality is, that person has been doing some serious behind-the-scenes work that has elevated them to that position. The energy and momentum behind their transformation was already flowing unseen for a while before the results became apparent, just as undercurrents in the ocean are powerful yet unobservable from the surface.

Take a deep breath and release any pressure you may feel to immediately quantum leap or run full speed ahead. Unless, of course, you live for speed. Then, by all means, do not let me slow you down! Do pace yourself, though, and listen to those who care about you when they express concerns that you may be going too fast too soon. True expertise takes time and experience, and that requires you to honor the space you are in. If you experienced your first reiki session yesterday and feel so excited about it that you now want to become a reiki master, that is amazing, but you will still need to take the time to really explore what it is, learn how to practice ethically, work on your skillset, and ensure you have the support needed to go all in. If you go full speed ahead without the right tools and foundation, and you are likely to crash and burn. I know this firsthand:

Several years ago, a successful business coach hired me to support her and her clients. We built her business to the highly-sought-after seven-figure mark within mere months of working together. She was brilliant at finetuning the systems needed to achieve this goal and had built a strong foundation and brand, and when we combined this with my intuition, ability to predict future trends, working with the energetics of a business, and a client-first approach, we quickly catapulted the company to new heights. It was so exciting to see the growth and potential we had created! We quickly started dreaming of what the next several years could look like and the impact we could make. However, the coach quickly became preoccupied with hypergrowth and to make as much money as quickly as possible, rather than to stabilize the business first. I watched the joy she had felt while helping others turn into an energy of "lack". This ultimately led to us parting ways. I knew that by giving our clients the attention they deserved and focusing more on their success, and worry less about hypergrowth, we would not only be just as successful, but we would also be happier and more fulfilled overall. However, she did not heed my plea to take the time to excel where we were at, put our clients who had already said yes to working with us as the top priority, and organically create more momentum.

I was unsurprised when I learned that her business had collapsed just a few months after my time ended.

I don't share this story to criticize, but to emphasize the importance of building alignment, finding balance, and making time to take a breath.

I share this cautionary tale not to discourage you from aiming to make quantum leaps in your life, business, career, or goals, but to advise you to do so from a foundation of your values, mission, and highest purpose (and with someone in your corner who is not afraid to hold up a mirror, when needed).

The alternative outcome of going too fast too soon is imposter syndrome. This is a psychological pattern in which an individual doubts their accomplishments, skills, or talents, and has a persistent internalized fear of being exposed as a "fraud" or as undeserving of their success. Sufferers often feel as though they do not deserve the recognition or opportunities they are given, and as a result, they flounder in feelings of inadequacy, self-doubt, and anxiety, even when they have made real accomplishments and repeatedly demonstrated their competence. Imposter syndrome is a common experience, and it can affect people in all fields at any stage of their career.

The best way to remedy this feeling or pattern (in my opinion) is to take a moment to be present, practice what you want to bring forward, and go all in on connecting with your highest self, so that you feel secure and confident in what you are delivering. Honor the space you are in without comparing your progress to anyone else's. Ask yourself if you are truly living and working in alignment with your values, or if there is an underlying motive that needs to be addressed before you move forward.

Rather than pushing exponential growth at hyperspeed for the sake of it or for material reasons (which may lead to a hollow outcome), I recommend that you first identify your zone of genius, and then apply the Kaizen principle, which I will outline on the next pages. You will see the success you desire *and* have the opportunity to grow with your vision. The genius zone concept will support you in finding balance and flow, while the Kaizen principle will allow you to form an approach to your goals that is more sustainable and kinder to your mental health and nervous system than the "full speed ahead" approach hustle culture promotes.

Creating from Your Genius Zone

Grace Lever, a successful entrepreneur and business coach, was the first person who introduced me to the idea of genius zones. This is an amazing concept that fosters sustainable transformation and allows you to live and create from a space of excitement and flow.

Your genius zone is that sweet spot where your passions, skills, and strengths align. When you work in your genius zone, tasks feel effortless, and time seems to fly by. It is the area in which you shine the brightest. It is in this space that you effortlessly tap into your strengths, leverage your talents, and channel your passions toward meaningful experiences.

Take a moment to reflect on your talents and what brings you joy. What are you naturally good at? What activities make you lose track of time? What tasks do others sometimes view as a chore, but you would love to do all day? These are clues that can guide you toward your genius zone.

When we engage in work that aligns with our strengths, we experience a state of flow. Flow is that wonderful feeling of being completely absorbed and focused on what you are doing. In this state, your productivity soars and you produce your best work. A Goddess knows that when she makes a conscious effort to work in her genius zone as much as possible, work feels lighter and more enjoyable, and success becomes a natural byproduct of her efforts.

Discovering and embracing your genius zone is not only about personal fulfilment. It is also about making a meaningful contribution to the world. What lights you up may be dreadful to another, and what you put off for weeks because it drains your energy, someone else is searching for opportunities to do! Once you release what is not in your field of alignment, you give someone else the opportunity to jump in and work within *their* personal zone of genius. In the words of Marie Forleo, another renowned entrepreneur and advocate for living our best lives, "True freedom and success come when you align your work with your true passions and operate in your genius zone. It's in that state of flow where you unleash your greatest potential and create magic."

For a while, I struggled to identify my genius zone. I am multi-passionate. I find that I can dabble in one area, such as writing, and then get bored and want to play in design. Then, I get tired of alone time and feel the urge to host a retreat so I can be in community with others. I have immensely enjoyed being a counselor, coaching others through yoga and meditation, and even working in sales and marketing. How could I identify my genius zone in a world with so many options?

One December afternoon, while I was meditating during a flight from Florida to Wisconsin, I received a divine download telling me that it was in the creation of retreats that my soul would find its purpose. This was a vision I had initially had over a decade prior, so I knew I had to heed this message. Since then, I have discovered that this download was absolutely correct. Through my retreats, I am able to touch upon many of the aspects of my skillset that I enjoy, such as sharing healing tools, leading meditations, researching the perfect place to host a retreat, and collaborating with other healers and guides. Before I could identify my genius zone, though, I had to first identify what I did *not* want to do.

What I knew for sure was I did not want to be stuck in an office job. I did not want someone else to dictate every minute of my schedule. I did not want to feel like I was wasting my time or talent. I did not want to run reports all day or spend hours on paperwork that could easily be done by an entry-level professional.

If you have not yet identified what you truly want, start with what you do not want or enjoy. This can give you some serious clarity regarding your personal genius zone.

In a similar vein, I have also learned that just because I *can* do something does not mean I should. For example, I *can* spend twenty hours creating a new webpage, or I can delegate that task to someone who can get it done in half the time (and enjoy the process far more than I would). I *can* take family photos on my own and spend thousands of dollars on camera equipment and dozens of hours on setting, lighting, and editing, or I can hire a professional who can do this all for a fraction of time and money and who is passionate about every step of the process. When I support other business owners in creating their own retreat, I remind them that they *can* spend dozens and dozens of hours researching the perfect location, planning the schedule, and finding collab partners, or they can hire me to put all the details together, saving a ton of time and creating an experience that is fun and enjoyable from beginning to end.

Finding your genius zone is a lifelong journey. As you evolve, your passions may shift, and new strengths may emerge. Embrace the process of growth and adaptation, and never be afraid to redefine your genius zone as you navigate the different stages of life.

It is also worth noting that your genius zone may or may not be something you are able to make into your main source of income. It is wonderful when things align that way, but it may be a passion project or side hustle instead. Perhaps it is something you slowly incorporate into a W-2 job, to give you more fulfilment and excitement in the work you are already doing. It is true that some decide to pursue an entrepreneurial path so they can make their genius zone their full-time gig, but you do not have to do this if it does not resonate. Not every woman desires that path, and there are many other ways in which you can lean into your genius zone. No matter what this looks like for you, your genius zone is the stuff that magic is made from, so it is certainly worth digging deeper to uncover. This is exactly what the women in my Goddess and Enchantment programs and retreats do.

Let's explore some techniques you can use to identify your genius zone and align your actions with your natural talents and abilities. The facts are, each one of us possesses unique strengths, talents, and passions that, when tapped into, can ignite a profound sense of purpose and fulfillment.

- Self-reflection and discovery. Take the time to reflect on your strengths and passions and what truly brings you joy. What activities make you lose track of time? What are you naturally good at? Do some journaling and seek feedback from those who know you best, to gain clarity on your unique abilities.
- Alignment of passion and purpose. Identify your passions and align them with a greater sense of purpose. What activities energize you

and make you feel alive? What impact do you want to make on the world?

- Growth and continuous learning. Explore opportunities to expand your knowledge, acquire new skills, and challenge yourself. By stepping out of your comfort zone, you stretch your abilities and unlock new dimensions of your genius. Remember, growth occurs when you push beyond the boundaries of what you already know. Try stepping out of your comfort zone to discover a new layer of your genius zone.

- Leverage your strengths. What comes naturally to you? What activities allow you to shine? By focusing on your strengths, you amplify your potential for excellence and find yourself in a state of flow more frequently. Reduce the time you spend on activities that block your flow. Delegate tasks that fall outside of your strengths to others who excel in those areas. This will allow you to maximize your impact and productivity and will bring your genius zone forth.

- Embrace challenges as opportunities. In your genius zone, challenges become steppingstones for growth and innovation. So, rather than avoiding or fearing challenges, embrace them as opportunities to learn, improve, and expand your capabilities. With the right mindset, challenges become catalysts for creativity and breakthroughs and often force you to play to your strengths. In other words, they call your genius zone forward.

- Create an environment for flow. When we minimize distractions, create a workspace that is conducive to flow, and establish routines that optimize focus and productivity, we "hyperspeed" our results in a sustainable way. So, bring things that inspire and motivate you into your space, such as meaningful affirmations, visual reminders of your goals, and a supportive network of likeminded individuals.

Identifying your unique abilities and what ignites your soul is exciting, isn't it? Even more exciting, your genius zones and opportunities for flow are not limited to any specific domain or profession; it is a universal concept that applies to all areas of our lives, whether our careers, hobbies, relationships, or personal pursuits. The key is to listen to your inner wisdom, honor your passions, and embrace the unique talents that make you who you are. The path to finding your genius zone may not always be linear, and it may require some courage along the way, but as you step into your brilliance, trust that the universe will conspire to support you and that your future self will thank you for taking the leap.

The Kaizen Principle

Have you ever skipped to the end of a novel, or jumped a season or two ahead of where you left off in a TV show, and nothing makes sense? *Why is he kissing that person? I thought they were enemies! When did they move to France? Where did her husband go?* Such questions lead you to enjoy the story less, until you can fill in the blanks. There are just too many gaps. Well, this is also the reason why we do not (and should not) know exactly what our future holds. Yes, we can visualize our future, ask for guidance about it, and even get clear downloads that manifest into reality, but what we do not have is a full, crystal ball view of all that our future will bring, and that is a good thing. Too much focus on the future robs you of present moment contentment and can lend the way to vertigo, disillusionment, or imposter syndrome when the future does arrive. This is also what happens when we focus on "hyperspeeding" our results: we miss the real juicy parts of our lives and risk looking back and wondering, *What just happened?*

Think of fast fashion and fast food. What is the first word that comes to mind when you think of these things? "Unsustainable"? "Unhealthy"? "Risky"? "Cheap"? I believe that the same sentiments apply to when we constantly dive headfirst into the next goal via the easiest, fastest route. When we do this, we bypass growth and healing. Skipping the line can feel good in the moment, but it ultimately leads to a lot of empty feelings, hurt people, and a wobbly foundation that is bound to crack in one way or another. I would therefore like to propose an alternative approach to goal achievement: the 1% Rule.

The concept of the 1% Rule, which you may already be familiar with, finds its roots in the Kaizen principle. So, let's explore that first.

The Kaizen principle is based on a Japanese management philosophy and was popularized by Masaaki Imai, an organizational theorist and management consultant, through his book *Kaizen: The Key to Japan's Competitive Success*. Kaizen, which is derived from the Japanese words *kai* (change) and *zen* (good), refers to the philosophy of continuous improvement. It emphasizes small, gradual change over time, to achieve significant progress. It focuses on steady, sustainable growth.

In a world driven by instant gratification and the desire for immediate results, it is easy to overlook the potential that lies within small, incremental change. The philosophy of Kaizen reminds us that lasting success and personal growth are often the result of consistent, continuous improvement. The application of this concept can lead to remarkable transformations that do not lead to burnout or spark massive imposter syndrome. Those first small steps toward your dreams may seem insignificant at first, but trust me, they create a ripple effect. Each step builds momentum, ignites your passion, fuels your determination, *and* brings you closer to those quantum leaps we spoke about earlier.

Kaizen is all about sustainable transformation that aligns with your values and reduces unnecessary stress and clutter. No more burnout or overwhelming pressure. With Kaizen, you can achieve lasting change while maintaining balance and self-care. This philosophy is a gentle reminder to be kind to yourself and to celebrate even the smallest victories. It encourages you to streamline processes, prioritize tasks, and work smarter, not harder. With each small step, you unlock a new level of greatness within yourself.

Your ego wants to keep you safe, while your inner Goddess wants to break free from the illusions of safety that come with playing small. Your ego believes that any change (even good change, which is exactly what Kaizen is) is a risk to your life. To quiet the ego-mind, move with intention and consistency. Show your ego that you are okay—better than okay—when you move toward your desires. By taking one small step each day toward your goals, you create a positive habit loop. These steps could be as simple as making a phone call you have been avoiding, researching new opportunities, or writing a few lines of the book that has been in the works for years.

A modern approach to Kaizen is the 1% Rule. Robert Maurer, PhD, a clinical psychologist and author of the book *One Small Step Can Change Your Life: The Kaizen Way,* is a notable proponent of the 1% Rule. In his book, Maurer explores the idea of taking small steps to work one percent closer toward lasting change and to overcome resistance to personal and professional growth. The 1% Rule is based around the premise that taking massive leaps all at once may not always be feasible or sustainable. If you want a life of passion, purpose, and full alignment with your highest self, it is essential to not push yourself to the brink of a breakdown (which is all too common in hustle culture). Sustainability is an act of self-love.

More than anything, the 1% Rule helps us to overcome resistance and fear. Taking small steps allows us to gradually expand our comfort zones and confront limiting beliefs that may otherwise hold us back. As we witness our ability to navigate through challenges and make progress, we develop resilience and a belief in our own capabilities. This empowers us to move beyond our perceived limitations and to strive for our truest desires.

The 1% Rule can also be a powerful tool for countering imposter syndrome and building confidence in oneself. When applied to imposter syndrome, the 1% Rule encourages individuals to focus on continuous improvement and progress, rather than perfection or comparison. By acknowledging that success is not about overnight transformations or immediate mastery, but consistent growth and incremental progress, the pressure to be flawless can be alleviated. After all, imposter syndrome often stems from the belief that one must meet incredibly high standards, or that one must be exceptional in every aspect of their work or life, to be deserving of success. The Kaizen or 1% mindset shift allows people to instead focus on personal growth and development, rather than constantly seeking external validation or comparing themselves to others. No two Goddesses are the same, and that's what makes everyone so magnificent!

When I was first starting my business while parenting three children under ten, I sometimes only had thirty minutes a day to create my coaching program, record a podcast, or connect with women who wanted to attend an event. However, by consistently dedicating a small portion of my time and energy to my aspirations, I ensured progress without overwhelming myself or neglecting my children in pursuit of worldly success.

Consistency is key when it comes to taking inspired action. So, commit to making progress every single day, no matter how small. Believe me, those small steps add up faster than you think! Rather than overwhelming yourself with the magnitude of the task or the fear of failure, break the goal down into manageable increments. By committing to taking just one percent of the necessary action each day, you can build momentum and create positive habits that spark momentum.

Moving Towards Your Dreams

Ever since I was very young, I always harbored a deep desire to become a successful writer and to share my stories with the world. I began this journey by writing a chapter in a collaboration book, which was an amazing feeling of accomplishment. It felt so surreal when my publisher sent the hardcopy to my home and equally incredible when it reached the bestseller list! The book that had been asking to be created was finally in my hands! I knew my next step was to write a solo book, as writing a book had been my dream since childhood. However, I often found myself overwhelmed by the enormity of this task. I stopped and started so many times and for so long that years went by. That is, until I applied the 1% Rule to my writing journey. Here, I made a commitment to myself: I would write just a fraction of my desired daily word count consistently, regardless of how busy or uninspired I felt.

At first, my efforts felt small and insignificant. Some days, it was a challenge to write even a few sentences. But I reminded myself that progress, no matter how small, was still progress. As I continued to write a little each week, I noticed a gradual change within myself. I was experiencing less and less resistance to the process of sitting down and writing. I became incentivized to develop a writing routine, and I created a dedicated space to write. Even on tough days, I was proud of the fact that I was showing up for my dreams, one small step at a time. Perhaps most importantly, I regularly reminded myself of my "why". I told myself about the women who were looking for the messages I was sharing in this book. I recalled how deeply I had once wished to find ways to reconnect with my higher self. I knew I could offer the women out there who had the same desire a guiding light to their life's purpose. I knew this book would become a source of inspiration for them as they learned to live in alignment with their dreams while nurturing their mind, body, and soul and practicing radical self-compassion.

Over time, my commitment to my "why" started yielding results. I grew more confident in my voice, and I grew more and more excited to share my insights. I even found myself feeling excited to write a little more than I'd initially promised myself I would each day. I did not want to stop once I got into the flow. By expanding my comfort zone and making more and more progress in the same amount of time the more I practiced, I reached a point where I could sit back and ride the momentum like a surfer riding a wave, resistance and procrastination a distant memory.

The Kaizen principle allowed me to break down my aspirations into manageable increments. This helped me overcome my fears and steadily move closer to my truest desires. As I write this, I will be sending the complete manuscript of this book to my publisher at the end of the week. The sense of pride and accomplishment I feel about that is nearly indescribable. I want the same feeling for you!

What small step can you take today to move one percent closer to your dreams?

The Beauty of Overflow

When you operate from your zone of genius, co-create sustainable transformation, and craft a life that embodies self-love and compassion, you create an overflow of abundance. The energy you exude keeps elevating and expanding until you eventually reach a state of magnificent overflow. Just as a downpour of rain provides enough water for a river to overflow, creating nourishment for the plants near the riverbanks and fresh movement for marine life, your lifeforce energy (or *chi*) flows out and through you to nourish your loved ones and your community.

Your highest self does not want you to suffer or to be in constant pain. While there will be times when you are stretched, uncomfortable, or feeling the burdens of the impermanent condition of the human body, you are designed to come back to a state of homeostasis (peace, clarity, ease, joy, and connection) in the end. Any other state of being is unnatural. This is why things feel so difficult and heavy when you are not in a state of flow and overflow. After all, when you are flowing, doesn't everything feel incredibly light and breezy? Maybe even playful and exciting?

We experience a block in our flow and, therefore, a block in the beauty of overflow when we are not operating in our genius zone, when we are placing too much pressure on results, or when we are constantly trying to "do it all and be it all."

I have a client who used to never ask for help. Her motto was, "I can do it better and faster myself." Perhaps you are someone who believes the same. Unfortunately, after years of trying to do everything on her own, she became completely burnt out. The exhaustion was taking a toll on her physical and mental health. This aggravated her, and at first, she blamed her job, her partner, and even her children. When I met her, she was close to calling it quits by changing careers and ending her marriage because she felt so unfulfilled. She said that it felt like no one cared about her or ever offered help.

Ding!

Did you hear that? Even though she pushed help away, deep down, she really desired their attention and help. But how would anyone in her life know that she really did want support? They believed that she *wanted* to do it all on her own, and more than likely, they could sense she would not trust them if they did offer a hand, or that she would maybe even criticize them if she felt that it was not up to her standards.

It all sounds so simple looking in from the outside, but I guarantee that each of us has similar tendencies in some areas of our lives. It is a natural consequence of us not taking the time to deeply listen and seek guidance from our higher selves.

Where in your life do you push help away? What areas could you use more assistance in? Are you overwhelmed by housework? If you live with others, enroll them into a team approach to keep the house clean and tidy, or hire a house cleaning service (what is overwhelming for you may be those professionals' zone of genius). You may first need to release any ideas of perfectionism you have, but once you do, you will be able to breathe easier knowing that not everything is on your shoulders. Do you have a business in which you are attempting to manage everything yourself? I have been a solopreneur (an entrepreneur who manages all the pieces of the business), so I understand the mind chatter that happens when you are considering hiring help. Maybe it is a VA or an editor that you need, but thoughts such as, *I can't afford help*, and, *It will take me longer to train someone than to just do it myself*, run rampant through your mind.

I get it. I have been there, too. Yet I also know the calm that comes from knowing that I am not alone and that I have people in my corner helping me to achieve that blessed state of flow and overflow. So, I ask again, what feels most overwhelming right now? Having consistent support is vital if you are to access your future self's gift of overflow, so take a moment to put a plan in place. Put your bookmark here and get on the phone or send an email. Ask for help and get referrals for a professional who can assist you with whatever your highest area of overwhelm is. Do you need a home organizer or housekeeper? A lawncare service? A video editor? A parenting coach? A nanny? A virtual assistant? Alternatively, speak with your existing family, friends, or team so you can take one thing off your plate today. Then, take a deep breath and allow the overflow of ease and gratitude to seep into your soul.

Alternatively, maybe you are in a moment of life in which you have extra time, resources, or a skillset that would be an invaluable support for another. I knew a woman, Beth, who was recently retired and whose grown children moved away, and she was feeling bored and a bit lonely. She realized that a friend of her daughter's needed childcare for date nights out with her husband (don't underestimate the little things that can make a big difference). Beth soon filled her metaphorical cup once a month with baby snuggles and board game adventures with the children, and even brought delicious homemade baked goods and a meal. The family began to invite her to birthday parties and special events. The family felt supported and functioned at a higher level by this seemingly simple gesture of lending a hand for a few hours a month, and it warmed Beth's heart to know that she had a role in helping the family flourish as well as enjoying the connections that she longed for. If you are in a state of being able to give support to another, take the time now to offer it, creating a win–win experience!

Goddess Inspiration: Amaterasu (Peace and Serenity)

Amaterasu is a Shinto Goddess who is considered to be the ancestor of the Japanese imperial family. In the rich history of Japanese mythology, she shines as the embodiment of the sun's brilliance. Amaterasu's energy is a serene dance of light and darkness, reminding us of the importance of finding equilibrium in our lives. Just as she illuminates the world with her radiant presence, she invites you to find the balance between your own light and shadow. Amaterasu also teaches us that true balance is not a static state, but a dynamic process that requires conscious awareness and constant adjustment.

Amaterasu reminds us to honor and embrace all aspects of our being; to recognize the importance of balancing the masculine (action) and feminine (receptive) energies within us; to respect the importance of both work and play.

To embody Amaterasu's essence, it is essential to cultivate a self-reflection and introspection practice. Regularly take the time to pause, assess, and reassess your priorities, actions, and energy distribution. Self-reflection allows you to gauge whether you are investing too much into one area of your life at the expense of another, and to make any necessary adjustments (to restore equilibrium). It also allows you to develop a deeper understanding of yourself and your needs, enabling you to navigate the ebb and flow of life with grace and equanimity. Recognize that overworking or neglecting rest can disrupt the delicate balance of your wellbeing and state of flow. When you prioritize self-care and allocate time for activities that nourish your body, mind, and spirit in both work and play, you infuse your life with vitality and fulfilment.

One way to assess how balanced your own life is, is to complete one of the fundamental practices of self-coaching, the Wheel of Life. If you are not familiar with the Wheel or have not completed one within the last six months, I highly recommend taking 30 minute to complete one this week, so you can better understand where you are achieving balance and which areas could use a little more attention. In the following "Inspired Action" section, I have included information on my personal take on the Wheel of Life.

Your life is meant to be in harmony, dear Goddess, so allow the influence of Amaterasu to inspire you to cultivate a life of sustainability and serenity. Know that it is through balance that you unlock the path to inner peace and deep fulfillment.

Inspired Action

Check out my Abundant Wheel of Life mini-course, created for you, dear Goddess, at www.goddessoflightretreats.com/wheel, so you can pinpoint the abundance that already exists in your life (even if you have not noticed it before) and address in detail the areas of your life where you could use more fulfillment.

5

Create

9

YOUR PLAN FOR INSPIRED ACTION

———

Energy flows where attention goes.
— Hawaiian Huna philosophy

AT THIS POINT, YOU SHOULD UNDERSTAND how to use your energy to co-create your personal legend, uplevel your wellbeing, and step into the identity of the woman you desire to be, *without* pushing yourself into a state of exhaustion. What's next?

Each of us has a unique purpose—a sacred path that calls us forward—and you already possess the strength and resilience to realize this purpose and manifest your deepest desires. If you did not, you would not have read this far. You cannot do this on autopilot, though. Therefore, as you navigate the complexities of life, it is crucial that you design a uniquely divine blueprint. This is an intentionally crafted plan for taking inspired action that guides you toward your destination.

Imagine someone preparing for a cross-country journey from the bustling, light-filled streets of New York to the sandy beaches of California for some much-needed sun, surf, and sand. Filled with excitement and anticipation, she sets off with no map in hand. She has decided she will trust only her instincts to guide her way. At first, the lack of direction seems liberating. It feels like an opportunity to surrender to the unknown.

However, as the miles pass by, she finds herself veering off-course, lost amidst the sprawling landscapes of Oklahoma. Eventually, she sits on the roadside in tears. She does not know which direction to go in. Not quite the dream vacation she planned, is it?

Similarly, if we do not take the time to craft a plan, we risk getting lost along our path, and we often fail to reach our intended destination. While it is true that life often surprises us with unexpected detours and scenic opportunities, having a plan serves as a compass and provides focus, direction, and a sense of purpose. We are more likely to get lost in confusion and overwhelm when we do not have at least a basic roadmap in hand. Just as a well-designed map leads you to your destination even when you experience bumps in the road, your divine blueprint ensures that you remain on-track even when you face challenges or moments of doubt. It becomes your guiding light, illuminating the path ahead and reminding you of the incredible potential that lies at the end of the journey. Of course, over time, you can add more details or allow yourself to adjust the sails in a different direction entirely, but having no plan of inspired action whatsoever is usually a recipe for unfulfillment.

What's more, creating your inspired action plan is an act of empowerment. Your inspired action plan is a declaration to the universe that you are committed to your dreams and that you are willing to put in the effort and dedication required to achieve them. By outlining your goals, breaking them down into actionable steps that align with your vision, and setting a clear timeline that holds space for both action and self-care, you take the reins of your destiny into your own capable hands. It also invites the universe to conspire in your favor. When you set your intentions and take inspired action, the universe aligns with your desires and helps to shape them into reality. In this way, the realization of your divine blueprint becomes a collaborative effort between you and the universe.

While your customized roadmap will prove invaluable, remember to embrace the joy of spontaneity and to allow yourself to venture off the beaten path from time to time. Life is filled with delightful surprises, and occasionally deviating from your plan when your higher self calls you to can lead to profound experiences and unexpected growth. Just as a traveler might decide to take a scenic detour to marvel at the beauty of their surroundings, you, too, can explore new avenues and savor the richness of the present moment.

While these detours can be invigorating, they can quickly become stressful and overwhelming without a plan to come back to. Like a car running out of gas or a flat tire without a spare, the absence of a well-defined plan can drain your energy and impede your progress. The exhilaration of the journey fades, leaving you stranded and unfulfilled. Alternatively, when you have your sights set on what you desire, you allow yourself to enjoy the ride with more fun and ease. With a clear roadmap in hand, you can anticipate potential roadblocks and navigate them.

Remember, the purpose of your plan is not to confine or limit you. It is to liberate and empower you. It grants you the freedom to dream big, envision the life you desire, and take decisive action toward its attainment. Studies conducted by psychologists and researchers have shown that when individuals take inspired action, they experience a boost in their overall wellbeing and satisfaction. Taking action that is aligned with one's desires not only propels them closer to their goals, but also instills a sense of purpose and fulfillment.

As you design your inspired action plan (we will be doing this in a moment), do not forget to invite divine guidance into the process. Ask for assistance from your inner Goddess, the universe, your spirit guides, or any higher power you resonate with. Trust in the power of your dreams, have faith in your ability to manifest them, and let your inspired action plan be your guiding light. Take comfort in the knowledge that you are well prepared for your journey to your personal legend and watch as the universe conspires to turn your dreams into a glorious reality.

Creating Your Blueprint

It is now time to begin the extraordinary adventure of designing your divine blueprint. During this process, we will tap into your superpowers, while keeping the journey light and joyous. Grab your favorite notebook and a cup of tea, and dive in when you are ready!

Step 1: Getting Clear on Your Vision

The first step to designing your intentional plan is getting crystal clear on what you truly want to create in your life. This involves connecting with your highest self (your inner Goddess) and allowing her to guide you toward your deepest desires (your north star).

Before we dive into the specifics, let's take a moment to set the stage. Find a quiet space where you can connect with your inner self. Light a candle or cleanse the room with sage, if you desire. Play some soft music without lyrics. Take a deep breath. Sit in stillness so you can listen closely to the whispers of your soul. This is a powerful practice that allows you to connect deeply with your highest self and tap into the wellspring of wisdom within you. Now, envision your most audacious goals. What do you desire to manifest in your life? Allow your imagination to run wild. Do not be afraid to dream big. Allow yourself to be the woman with lofty dreams and aspirations. Embrace the stillness around you and listen closely to the whispers of your inner guidance. What is it that truly ignites your spirit? Write down your aspirations with as much detail as possible. They will serve as the guiding stars in your journey. Allow yourself to remain open to the genius, power, and magic that will arise.

Step 2: Planning Your Inspired Action

Now that you have defined your dreams and goals, it is time to step into inspired action. Break down your goals into smaller, manageable steps. Think of these steps as little adventures you will go on. Imagine you are a treasure hunter and that each action step takes you closer to the rare and valuable gems you seek. Allow yourself to feel giddy excitement and anticipation as you write down these steps. It is okay to use colorful markers or to doodle little smiley faces on your blueprint. Let your inner child have some fun!

If you do not break your dreams down into manageable pieces and take intentional action, your dreams will likely remain just a distant fantasy. If you learn to enjoy the process of shaping a detailed plan and considering each step needed to bring your dream to life, however, you may find yourself amazed at how much you can accomplish with joy and ease. Setting realistic deadlines for these steps will ensure you have ample time to accomplish each task without overwhelm. To reduce the likelihood of falling into a state of distress and ultimately giving up on the journey, make a conscious effort to dedicate your full attention to each action you take and follow it through.

Consider what steps are needed to achieve your goal. You might put your action steps on a timeline of events, use sticky notes on a wall, or create a new Trello board. Consider giving yourself a full hour or two to dive deep into all the micro-actions that need to be taken in order to achieve the big goal. For example, when planning a retreat, I know that I need to find a location, determine if I will have co-hosts and who they will be, finalize the dates, and make a general budget; next, I plan activities; then I further align the budget to what activities, meals, and other expenses will be; then I create a marketing plan with emails and social media to get the word out; next I potentially create partnerships... the list goes on. (And it's a long list, which is why I also help provide a roadmap to those who desire to create a retreat themselves, or to plan the whole enchilada for businesses and leaders who want a done-for-you service). My point being that if you don't do this step with a high level of intention, you risk missing some very important pieces which may lead the entire goal to crumble—and I want to see you succeed, so do this step, Goddess!

Step 3: Nurture Your Sacred Space

In the process of designing your inspired action plan, it is crucial to cultivate a nurturing and supportive environment that uplifts and empowers you. The surroundings in which you immerse yourself and the people around you can have a profound impact on your wellbeing and your ability to manifest your dreams. To cultivate a nurturing environment, begin by seeking out communities or groups that resonate with your goals and aspirations. Connect with individuals who uplift and inspire you; who genuinely support your journey and cheer you on. Engage in conversations and attend workshops, Goddess circles, or retreats, or join online forums where you can share your dreams and learn from others who are on a similar path. Also seek out mentors or role models who embody the qualities or achievements you aspire to have. Their guidance and wisdom can provide valuable insights and help you to navigate the challenges and uncertainties that may arise along your journey. When we surround ourselves with likeminded individuals who share our vision, or with mentors who have walked a similar path, we enter a world of support, encouragement, and inspiration.

Once you have your support circle in place, dedicate some time to creating a physical space that reflects your aspirations and serves as a sanctuary for your growth and wellbeing. Consider decluttering and organizing your environment to create a sense of peace and clarity. Infuse your space with things that inspire you, such as artwork, plants, or meaningful objects. Surround yourself with visual reminders of your dreams and the possibilities that lie ahead, to plant the seeds of the visualization process in a very organic way.

By consciously creating a nurturing and supportive environment and embracing the power of community, you are creating the fertile ground needed for your dreams to take root and blossom into reality. What needs to be done now for you to have the space and support to align with your visions?

Step 4: *Leaning Into the Magic of Surrender and Flow*

While inspired action is crucial, it is equally important to embrace the magic of surrender. Surrender is the art of releasing control and trusting in the divine flow of life. This is sometimes the most difficult thing to do, especially for high-achieving women! Surrender becomes a natural byproduct of the profound realization that you are co-creating with the energy that created everything, and that the universe has a plan that is far greater than anything you can comprehend. Surrender is not about giving up or being passive; it is about letting go of resistance and embracing the natural currents of life. To cultivate surrender, practice releasing attachment to specific outcomes. Trust that the universe knows the desires of your heart and will guide you to the highest and most fulfilling path. Be open to receiving unexpected opportunities and guidance that may lead you to even greater heights than you ever envisioned you would go to. (If you ever need more targeted guidance on how to get into a state of flow, please do revisit the previous chapter).

As we have touched on previously, it is essential for you to honor both your feminine energy (which is grounded in trusting your intuition, taking time to rest, and finding comfort in connecting to people and nature) and your masculine energy (which is drawn to creating a plan, and then a backup plan, and to be on the move). The Goddesses of the past and the modern female leaders we look up to today showcase that when we balance these two energies (the yin and the yang), we can reach our destination with more joy, ease, and grace.

Adaptability is essential when you are curating the life you desire, and it is through surrender and a deep attunement to the present moment that you can discover the hidden treasures concealed within the ebb and flow of the cosmic tides. When you truly lean into this way of living, you quickly discover that change is not a threat, but a gateway to spiritual growth and expansion.

Life often throws curveballs into our plans. We may find ourselves stuck in cycles we thought we had already broken, or in situations we would never wish upon anyone, or experiencing the lowest lows that we could ever imagine. Knowing in advance that our plans will likely go off-track sometimes will prepare us to give ourselves compassion and grace when it happens. But we also need the drive to come back after we dust ourselves off. Sometimes, we even need to give ourselves the permission to map out an entirely new path altogether, and to embody the essence of the resilient and adaptable Goddess within. Surrender will allow you to let go of stress, anxiety, and the need to control every aspect of your journey, and it will create space for miracles and divine intervention.

Step 5: Celebrate Every Step of the Journey

How often do you make huge strides in your goals, and not acknowledge it?

Along your path, remember to celebrate every step of the journey, no matter how small it may seem. Acknowledge your progress, honor your commitment to yourself, and revel in the joy of becoming the architect of your own destiny. Actively express gratitude for the lessons you have learned and the growth you have experienced. By celebrating each milestone, you infuse your journey with the momentum needed to keep going. These celebrations can be as simple as a joyful dance, or as elaborate as a spa day. The most important thing is to acknowledge and appreciate the progress you have made. If you are feeling really adventurous, invite your friends or family to join in the celebration. Dance together, laugh together, and create a collective vibration of joy and accomplishment.

Take a moment to think about the ways in which you love to celebrate and be acknowledged. A soak in a candlelit bath of Epsom salts and essential oil? A new colorful dress? Or maybe a dinner out with the hubby or bestie?

For some women, self-rewarding feels uncomfortable, because they have been taught to be humble and, ultimately, to be taken for granted. Yes, you read that right: women have been conditioned, historically, to be used and taken for granted. But this shall happen no more, because we are bringing back Goddess energy!

Be your biggest cheerleader, even if it feels like no one else is in your corner. Set yourself up for the win, praise yourself when you accomplish a goal, allow your heart to sing when you are proud, and show yourself compassion when you fall. Remember, there is no failure in this experience called life. We just go forward and start again, this time with more wisdom, clarity, and confidence now that we have experienced a new stumbling block. If we need to rest, we take a break and then forge ahead, refreshed and raring to go.

In the *Inspired Action* section of this chapter I have shared ideas on how you can celebrate your accomplishments. From simple, no-cost activities you can do at home to larger more extravagant celebrations, the list will help you develop more motivation to keep reaching towards your dreams. Your future self wants to celebrate with you, so let's keep going!

Step 6: Self-Care is the Secret Ingredient

Every time I listen to a million-dollar business owner list the critical elements that helped them to achieve their highest potential, they never fail to include sleep, hydration, exercise, and leisure time as essential elements to success. If you do not address your basic human needs *and* add a good dose of fun into your life, your tank will eventually run out before you reach your desired destination. So, as you follow your plan for inspired action, remember that while your plan is your map, self-care is your fuel. Take breaks when you need them, nurture your mind, body, and spirit, engage in activities that bring you joy and recharge your energy, and sprinkle some laughter into your approach. Do not neglect to create moments in which you can walk barefoot on the earth, take a swim in a river, or breathe in the fresh air during a nature walk. Nature is a potent elixir for the soul, fueling your journey with renewed vitality.

Self-care is a deeply personal practice that is unique to each individual. It can encompass a range of activities, from physical exercise and nutrition to mindfulness practices, creative outlets, and spiritual rituals. The key is to carve out dedicated time for self-care and to treat it as a non-negotiable aspect of your daily routine. The positive impact of self-care on overall life satisfaction, resilience, and goal achievement is astronomical. When you prioritize your wellbeing, you replenish your energy, enhance your focus, and cultivate a sense of inner harmony. It is from this place of alignment that you can fully show up for yourself and your dreams.

I have learned firsthand that the foundation for sustainable success is formed when you meet your basic needs. It is like building a skyscraper: you cannot have a strong and towering structure without a solid foundation. So, eat nourishing foods that fuel your energy and support your wellbeing, create moments of rest and rejuvenation, and honor the need for adequate sleep and relaxation. I cannot stress enough how important this is. Your body is your vehicle. So, engage in activities that make you feel vibrant and alive! If you are not someone who loves working out but you want to reap the physical and mental benefits of movement, incorporate into your routine activities you enjoy, such as yoga, dancing, or kayaking. Join a local tennis club or plug a swim into your calendar every week. Exercise can be made genuinely enjoyable if you find a form that aligns with you (and that does not feel like work!).

Equally important is tending to your mental and emotional wellbeing. The ideas I included in earlier chapters (such as cultivating a mindfulness practice, meditation practice, or deep breathing practice) are great ways to do this. Make space for quiet and introspection, as well as activities that bring you joy and help you release stress. Don't underestimate the importance of laughter and connection! Seeking support from therapists, coaches, or trusted friends who can provide guidance and a safe space for emotional expression will also pay dividends as you step out your comfort zone and into the highest version of yourself.

Nurturing your spiritual connection with yourself is also a transformative aspect of self-care. Engage in practices that resonate with your soul, such as prayer or meditation. Connect with nature daily. By embracing self-care and cultivating inner alignment, you honor yourself and create a solid foundation for the manifestation of your personal legend.

Step 7: Cultivate Gratitude

It is through gratitude that you align yourself with the abundant, flowing energy of the universe. This allows miracles to unfold and blessings to manifest in your life.

Cultivating gratitude has transformative effects on our overall wellbeing and happiness. By focusing on the blessings and abundance that surrounds us, we shift our perspective and invite more blessings into our lives. Gratitude creates a magnetic field that attracts positivity and abundance.

Cultivating gratitude starts with developing a daily practice of counting your blessings. So, take a moment each day to reflect upon the gifts, big and small, that have graced your life. Write them down in a gratitude journal, speak them aloud, or offer silent prayers of gratitude to the divine. By acknowledging and appreciating the abundance already present in your life, you open the floodgates to even more blessings. Eckhart Tolle, a renowned spiritual teacher, reminds us, "Acknowledging the good that you already have in your life is the foundation for all abundance." I accordingly invite you to make gratitude a way of life. Each day, embrace the blessings that surround you, and trust in the divine orchestration of your journey as you open yourself up to the infinite possibilities and miracles that await you. When your heart overflows with gratitude, you watch as your path unfolds with divine grace and synchronicity, leading you toward a life filled with abundant blessings and profound joy.

By engaging in practices that I have outlined throughout this book, you will release a plethora of feel good hormones which will help you even further align with your future self's path. Which self-care and gratitude practices will you infuse into your daily and weekly routine?

Goddess Inspiration: Saraswati (Creativity and Self-Expression)

Saraswati is a Hindu Vedic Goddess associated with creativity, wisdom, music, and the arts. She is depicted as a serene figure playing the veena (a musical instrument). Her name means "elegant" and "flowing", and she is symbolized as a sacred river.

Creativity is essential for survival. It is the breath of the soul and the heartbeat of the universe. As you awaken our creative powers, the universe dances in joy, inviting you to become more aware of the potential that resides within. So, to kickstart your journey, please release the idea that in order to be creative, you must be crafty, or have art hung on your walls. While I have many friends who are incredibly artistic, creativity is about who we are, not what we do, and it is not confined to a specific medium or talent. It is a way of life. It means infusing each moment with imaginative flair. From writing to painting to plating a meal to problem-solving, every action offers an opportunity for you to express your creative essence. During your daily life, allow yourself to play, experiment, and explore new avenues of self-expression.

Take a moment to consider what your favorite ways to express your creativity are. Some of you will say, "But, Marie, I'm not creative!" but I call nonsense! You are. What's more, by nurturing your creative spirit, you align yourself with a deeper sense of purpose and fulfillment. Saraswati reminds us to listen to our intuition and honor our passions; to trust in our own unique paths and to let creativity be our guide. When we align our actions with our innermost desires, we create a life that resonates with authentic joy and expression.

I spent a year as a coach in Michelle Baker's "Art as a Soul Language" program, and was awestruck by the transformations that occurred when the women dug deep into their hearts and souls to produce a work of art that captured their life stories. They became more aligned with their truest selves, their deepest desires, and even their greatest fears. Each woman was guided in a journey to use her creative powers to discover what her soul needed her to see.

There are infinite ways in which you can open your creative channels. Any activities that spark a feeling of free expression or passion are their own form of creativity. I, for one, *must* create. It reminds me of why I am alive. Without self-expression, I feel stagnant and restricted. It is almost like I am suffocating. When I am dancing, painting, writing, traveling, or playing, passionate energy runs through my cells, and any challenges that arise seem less burdensome. A sense of ease, clarity, and purpose bubbles up and replaces fear and worry.

Do you remember that the sacral chakra (the space for creativity) resides in the womb? This is not an accident or coincidence. Even love-making is a form of creative expression!

As you dive into creative pursuits, you will witness a remarkable shift in your confidence. The act of bringing your unique ideas and visions to life empowers you to step outside your comfort zone and take bold risks. You may even find yourself wanting to share your creative side with others, since it is the purest expression of your authentic essence. Lean into Saraswati's guidance as you explore the depths of your imagination and discover the beauty of self-expression that resides within you. Saraswati reminds us that our voices are valuable, and that when we share our ideas, thoughts, and stories, we inspire and uplift others. By connecting with this essence, we can overcome self-doubt, fear, and societal constraints, embrace the power of self-expression, and use our voices to make a positive impact in the world. Trust in your ability to create and express yourself authentically, regardless of whether your creativity would be condoned or not by your fifth grade art teacher!

Inspired Action

Make a list of fifty-two ways in which you enjoy celebrating. Yes, fifty-two! I want you to get into the habit of celebrating yourself on a regular basis. If you are not acknowledging your wins at least weekly, it is hard to keep your cup full and to feel inspired to keep making progress on your inspired action plan. I suggest you make most of these ideas practical and cost effective, but go ahead and add a few that completely light you up and feel a touch extravagant.

Your highest self will revel in this praise and keep sending your opportunities and messages that will allow you to rise higher and higher on this amazing path of inspired action.

If you need help with this list, I have made a "cheat sheet" of sorts for you! You can go download the "52 Goddess Celebrations" at www.goddessoflightretreats.com/celebrate for a variety of ways how you can celebrate you!

CREATING A TIMELESS LEGACY

―――

"When you live with authenticity and follow your heart, you create the life
you are meant to live, and that becomes your legacy."
—Sarah Ban Breathnach

CONGRATULATIONS, GODDESS! WHAT A BEAUTIFUL JOURNEY you have been cultivating as you have been healing, aligning, amplifying, flowing, and creating! You have claimed your intentions, began the process of becoming the woman of your dreams, and began your journey on a path that will lead you to your purpose and your deepest desires. You have chosen to step into the fullness of your divine potential. You have explored the importance of creating community with your fellow sisters, recognizing that your strength multiplies when you rise together. You have discovered that the collective magic women hold empowers us all, igniting a universal fire that benefits all of us. Along this sacred expedition, you have embraced the power of radical self-love and compassion, for it is through nurturing yourself that you unlock the full radiance of your Goddess essence. You have celebrated your strengths and your imperfections, knowing that they are part of the art that makes you unique and magnificent through the brilliance of the philosophy of Wabi Sabi.

As you finish this book, I invite you to not view this as an ending, but as just the beginning for all the goodness that awaits you. May the ripple effects of our journey together touch the lives of countless others, inspiring them to rise, embrace their divinity, and believe in the power of their dreams. Together, as a collective force of powerhouse women, we become the catalysts for a world where every woman stands firmly in her power and co-creates a harmonious and abundant reality for herself and those around her.

As you continue to receive messages from your future self, may you continue to trust that divine spark that resides within you always. May your journey be filled with sacred connection, inspired action, and unwavering self-love.

Embodying Your Goddess Energy

I hope you enjoyed the Goddess Inspiration sections at the end of each chapter of this book. It was so fun to consider how each Goddess's energy flows and how we can use these archetypes to inspire our own co-creation journeys.

I do have one more Goddess whose essence I desire to share with you before we say goodbye for now. I believe this Goddess brings all the pieces we have explored together. We will talk about this Goddess at the end of this chapter.

Some of the Goddesses we have explored together may have felt closely connected to you. Others may have felt like strangers who you were curious to learn more about. Either way, the Goddesses we have explored in this book only scratch the surface of the Goddess energy available to every one of us. How exciting is that? Feel free to delve further into learning about the Goddesses we explored as well as the countless additional women who have set the stage for us to lean into our individual and collective strength, love, and beauty.

As we are all interconnected across time and space, you may resonate with powerful women or Goddess archetypes who are, or are traditionally depicted as being, of a different race or belief system to you. I assure you that this is common and completely okay. You are not culturally or spiritually appropriating Goddess wisdom when you enter this realm with a pure heart, an open mind, and the utmost respect for the challenges that the women you are drawn to have faced historically (and that their lineages or respective cultures may continue to face in our modern times). I believe that knowledge and compassion are tools that can move us all into a state of more equality and justice.

This in mind, consider which Goddess we have talked about in this book that you feel you already embody. Which one aligns most closely with your essence and strengths at this moment in time? Did you feel your body being drawn to one or two women in particular? Embrace that feeling of connection and celebrate the qualities you already possess. Take out your journal and write what moved you to choose this Goddess. What characteristics does she possess that align with your current state of being? You may even wish to conduct more thorough research into her background, so you can feel closer to her.

Next, ponder which of the Goddesses you desire to bring more of into your life. Is it the compassionate and enlightened nature of Kuan Yin that calls to your soul? Perhaps it is the fiery and transformative energy of Pele that ignites your passion for change. Call upon the Goddess who resonates deeply with your aspirations and allow her essence to guide you on your journey of personal growth and empowerment. Write about what captivates you about her, or even invite her essence to move through you as you dance to music that harnesses the power of the Goddesses.

Remember as you listen to messages from your future self that you have the incredible opportunity to draw wisdom and inspiration from these strong and bold characters of the past. They can serve as allies, guiding lights on your path, and sources of strength and empowerment. Their stories and qualities can be woven into your own unique story, vision, and strengths. Let their wisdom fuel your own pursuit of abundance, fulfillment, passion, and purpose. As I keep reiterating, you have the power to co-create your journey, infusing it with the wisdom and strength of these Goddesses while honoring your own individuality and intentions.

As you move forward, know that you are a divine being who is capable of greatness and who has infinite possibilities before her. You are a Goddess in your own right. Your journey awaits, and the Goddesses are walking beside you every step of the way.

Continue the Journey

If you are yearning for a deeper immersion into your sacred journey, I invite you to join me at a transformational retreat, a VIP experience, or one of the programs or memberships I have intentionally curated for women like you, who are ready to take inspired action and be in a community of empowered women. In this sacred space, we delve into the depths of our divine power, explore the wisdom of our highest selves, and elevate the energy from within through beautiful, holistic practices—with a touch of adventure, of course! We create spaces of vulnerability, healing, and support where women can come together and share their stories.

Alternatively, if you feel called to share your own sacred space with others, I am here to support you in that journey, too. I can guide you in creating and facilitating your own transformative retreat or circle, where you will serve as a light for others who are seeking to reclaim their power.

If you feel a calling to join me on this journey—to step into your role as a catalyst for change—I invite you to reach out. Together, we can co-create magnificent opportunities for empowerment. When we unite, we create an unstoppable force of love and transformation. Choose your adventure. Take inspired action. And always remember, you are a Goddess in human form worthy of all the beauty and joy that life has to offer!

Goddess Inspiration: Xochiquetzal (Sensuality and Beauty)

In the enchanting mythology of the Aztecs, the Goddess Xochiquetzal reigns as a radiant symbol of feminine power, beauty, and sensual allure. True beauty radiates from within, rooted in self-acceptance and self-love, and by connecting with the essence of Xochiquetzal, you become a vibrant embodiment of inner beauty, captivating others with your unique radiance and light.

Embodying Xochiquetzal's essence means living with the full sensual expression of your *shakti* (your feminine power) and feeling your *prana* (lifeforce energy) awaken from within and move throughout your entire physical and energetic body.

Sensuality is often misunderstood as sexuality. While there is an overlap between the two, they are not one and the same. Sensual expression is the art of connecting deeply to your senses. It is the practice of immersing yourself in the textures, scents, tastes, sounds, and sights that create a profound experience of pleasure and connection with yourself and the world around you.

When you embrace your innate sensuality, you may also become more open to engaging in sexual pleasures as well, but this is because you now have the knowledge of what makes you melt and surrender—what brings you the most pleasure—not because sensuality and sexuality are the same thing.

To fully embody the essence of Xochiquetzal and embrace your sensuality, I encourage you to engage in activities that make you feel beautiful and sexy. Explore the art of sensual dance, such as belly dancing, salsa, or pole dancing. Allow your body to move with grace and confidence. Welcome the natural rhythms and curves that make you uniquely captivating.

Alternatively, consider indulging in body painting, using vibrant colors and intricate designs to adorn your skin. In this way, you can celebrate your body as a canvas of beauty and self-expression. If you have a partner to explore with, take turns brushing body paint on each other while expressing what you admire about one another. If your partner would not be open to this experiment, no problem! Do this for you and allow them to change their mind and join you later.

Another delightful way to awaken your senses and reconnect with your sensuality is to create a sensual bath experience. Fill your tub with warm water, add luxurious essential oils that evoke your desired mood, scatter fragrant flower petals, dim the lights, and play soothing music. Allow yourself to be immersed in this sensuous sanctuary, feeling the caress of water on your skin, inhaling the intoxicating scents, and surrendering to the pleasure of the present moment. Allow your hands to glide over any parts of your body that you have been reluctant to touch, or even to allow a lover to touch. What if these parts are also part of the gorgeous, radiant whole that deserves appreciation?

Embodying your sensuality is a personal journey, and there are countless ways in which you can cultivate and celebrate it. Explore activities that resonate with you, whether having a sensual massage, wearing beautiful lingerie, or simply taking the time to gaze at your reflection in the mirror with love and admiration. The key is to identify what makes you feel beautiful and sexy. This opens your awareness to the plethora of senses in your body and honors your unique expression of your sensuality. Through these practices, you will deepen your connection with the essence of Xochiquetzal.

Xochiquetzal's energy reminds you that your physical and sensual experiences can be sacred and empowering. Just as she embodies the blossoming of flowers and the allure of nature, she invites you to embrace your own sensuality and to honor your body as a sacred temple. Sensuality is a natural expression of your lifeforce energy and should be celebrated and cherished. This Goddess's essence encourages the practice of self-love and self-acceptance and believes everybody should embrace and honor the beauty and uniqueness of their own body without fear or shame. Embrace the beauty of every curve, every stretch mark, and every nuance that makes your body unique. The way your body moves, dances, and breathes creates a symphony of grace and resilience.

Inspired Action

Ready to step fully into your most radiant self? I invite you to join me to go even deeper on your journey; to lean all the way into radical self-compassion; to step into your most courageous and empowered self; to use visualization to become the woman of your dreams; to design your personal inspired action plan; and create a timeless legacy; all while continuing to be inspired by Goddess energy and to fully embrace your own inner Goddess.

I would also love to see you on a future retreat with me and other Goddesses. Head to www.goddessoflightretreats.com for my current events and programs. This is only the beginning of your journey.

BONUS CHAPTER
WISE WOMAN MESSAGES

———

THIS CHAPTER IS DEDICATED TO THE women who have been through the depths of life's shadows and still returned to the light; to the women who are committed to being part of the solution as they listen to the wisdom of their highest self and live from a place of passion and purpose. I present the insights of such women to you as bonus Goddess messages, for we each have the capacity to activate the highest potential within one another.

Goddess Star

It was pitch dark. I was frozen, and I could not breathe. The sound of my heartbeat was deafening. My ribcage felt like a crushing prison as my heart tried to beat itself out of its prison and into freedom. *Beat beat beat. Beat-beat-beat. BEAT-BEAT-BEAT.* I was drowning in overwhelm.

Then, a hand touching mine.

Then, a sound.

A voice saying, "I'm here. You're okay."

Air. I gasped for air. I released a shuddering breath. And then another. And another.

I was not alone. There was a guide in the darkness, specifically assigned to me. *I was not alone.*

I learned through that experience to reach out, ask for help, and trust that even in the darkness, there is a guide who has been specifically assigned to me. I learned to trust that in the darkness, love is still reaching for you, always. When constriction comes, breathe and breathe again. Love is reaching for you.

—STAR THOMAS-WYSE, Wisdom Coach, Author, and Akashic Records Channel, Missouri (USA)

Goddess Lydia

An obstacle is not an invitation to push harder but an inquiry to go to your deepest depths. Get quiet. Close your eyes. Take a deep breath and ask, "What is it I need to know in this moment?" If you're doubting yourself, always run wildly in the direction of your desires. When you're lit up, you attract others who are lit up. You were born a magical being and always have access to the truest part of who you are. Above all, trust your MAGIC.

—LYDIA MANDELL, Breathwork Facilitator and Embodiment Guide, Connecticut (USA)

Goddess Elaine

You are worthy. Be patient with yourself and others without judgment. Breathe deeply and savor each moment. Keep dancing and nurturing your passions. Prioritize self-love and self-care every day. Make decisions from a place of joy, not fear. Trust your intuition, your spirituality, and the presence of angels. Make safe choices. Acquire and value property. You are destined to inspire yourself and others to greatness by sharing your gifts.

—ELAINE GRIGGS, Founder of CS4Youth, Maine (USA)

Goddess Robin

You were never a mistake, and you did not arrive by accident. It took two hundred and fifty-four people in just the last eight generations to survive for you to be here just as you are right now. You were put in all the right places and spaces on purpose so you could bring light and awareness, not so you could merely belong. You were never meant to be just like everyone around you. Your desire to leave this earth as you walked through the deepest valleys of your life was your soul begging you to listen and acknowledge your gift (not your curse) of uniqueness. Your ability to learn and know this without a doubt is your very key to freedom, and this is exactly why you are here on Earth right now. It is why you have remained here for all these years. You were put here on purpose. There were no accidents involved in your existence.

—ROBIN L. HOUSER, Mental Health Therapist, Iowa (USA)

Goddess Rachel

Dearest One,

I know sometimes you feel that life has passed you by. If you only you could find the lost key to understanding it all. I know you are not sure if you are doing the right thing. You are worried about your future. I know that you wonder whether the people around you will ever see the real you. Your heart longs to be free from the layers of grief and shame you carry. With tears of joy in my eyes, I want you to know that you do find the key. Keep asking the Universe for help. She provides! All that your soul desires comes to pass, and better than you could possibly imagine. You find great love. You become fully healed. You embody your destiny as a leader and beacon for so many, all because you never gave up on yourself. I am so proud of you, and I am cheering you on, my love. You are divine.

—RACHEL CHASE, Founder of Rachel's Healing Arts, Washington (USA)

Goddess Dezarrea

We only get one shot at this thing called Life. Tomorrow isn't promised, so let's make every day count. My mom taught me that it's better to give than to receive and so my mission is to make my life about finding ways to give, and every time I give, it comes back tenfold. Let's focus our attention on how we can be a help to others. Everyday that I am here on earth is a blessing and I don't want to take it for granted! Live your best life now!
—DEZARREA KINDLE, Realtor/Owner, Wisconsin (USA)

Goddess Sonia

Stay grounded in your body, Goddess!
—SONIA RENE, Founder of Wild Creative, Louisiana (USA)

Goddess Kellie

I know you have had your doubts and fears, and yet you have persevered and pushed through. And now, here you are, enjoying the fruits of your commitment and love for learning. Your passion to help and succeed inspires many women who have watched your journey and your transformation into the best version of yourself.

You are where you are meant to be, and you belong in this space. Seize the opportunities that come your way. You have a voice and a story that many women can resonate with. Own both your success and failure. Be your true, authentic, best self. Show up every day. Your voice matters. Your story matters. You matter.
—KELLIE SABAS, Founder of HappyME.yoga, Manila (Philippines) & California (USA)

Goddess Julie

The experience of Heaven lies within you and requires no perfection. You create your Heaven on Earth. Heaven is not a place beyond your knowing;

it is experienced in each breath, even as you read this. It is the attitude you hold. It is a mindset. It is a shift in perspective. Heaven exists in every choice you make, day in and day out. It is the output of your soul's rhythm. It is in the smell of the lilacs in springtime and the dance of leaves in the wind during the fall. It is in the sound of a baby crying. It is in a smile from a stranger. It is found in every interaction you have. You walk in Heaven daily, and your light inspires others to do the same.

Always remember, you choose to create your Heaven on Earth. You are Heaven.

—JULIE LYNN GYGER, Wisconsin (USA)

Goddess Cindy

Years ago, my self-worth was nonexistent. I would constantly think, *Who am I? I am not good enough. I can never live up to anyone's expectations.* If only I had searched for help sooner, be it counseling, books, friends, or God. When we reach a crisis point, there are always so many signs pointing us in the right direction. Plus, we are blessed with sisters—other women—to learn from and to give to.

Wisdom and love come from so many different places. Open your heart, mind, and soul. Listen and act. I learned more than I could ever have dreamed of from my children and my grandchildren, once I started listening.

If you are blessed with courage and confidence, reach out to others with less. If you lack courage and confidence, reach out and ask for help. You are worth it. Find your strength. Be kind and compassionate. Bring that inner Goddess from within out for all to see!

—CINDY L. ALLEN, *Marie's Mom*, Florida (USA)

Goddess Kira

You know that warm feeling you get when you are overflowing with love for someone in your life, because you see them? You see their light through the darkness they are in, and so you show them grace when they are vulnerable. You speak kindness and compassion into them. In these moments, you find it so easy to give and pour into others. Yet, when it comes to you giving and pouring into yourself, you say, "I'll make time for me tomorrow." You look at the list of things you need to do tomorrow and you realize you are too busy for yourself, so you promise you'll get to caring for you the next day. Surely you can find time for you somewhere. The time never seems to come. Instead you find that there's more projects so you can help and care for everyone and everything around you. You notice at some point, exhausted, burned out, raw, that in doing so much for everyone else, you have forgotten you are worthy of that same love. You, my love, deserve to experience *you* and the absolute depths of your heart and soul; the joy, the sorrow, the beauty, the grief. You deserve to experience yourself, in every single facet of your incredible existence. You, your being, the way you radiate love, is a gift. It is time to give yourself permission to love on yourself in the ways you so magnificently love on others.

—KIRA GABRIEL, Founder of The Sable Moon, Illinois (USA)

Goddess Louise

In times of tears, when hopelessness and powerlessness have settled like a parasite onto your spirit, an ember of hope glows dimly within. This light cannot be extinguished. It is an innate "knowing" that you belong, are unconditionally loved, and are powerful.

You have a unique role to play in the story of your family line and within humanity. Whether that role is to break generational traumas, add to the human compendium of knowledge, care for your community, or innovate positive social change in the world, you are here to express and liberate yourself and the collective, fully.

What's more, you are only here for a single chapter in the story of humanity. Your ancestors have written the chapters that came before you, and they now support you in writing yours.

Will your chapter be authentically you and beneficial for future generations? Will future readers look back and be proud or thankful for your chapter? Will you be a good ancestor?

Your chapter matters. *You* matter!

In times of tears, remember this ember. Stoke it into a fire. Feel its warmth and light. Scare the hopelessness and powerlessness away from your spirit. It cannot exist in the light.

—LOUISE O'REILLY, Inclusion, Diversity, Equity & Allyship Coach, Perth (Australia)

Goddess Maren

Grace. It all comes down to grace. Grace for myself, for my mistakes, my mishaps, the thoughts and feelings I thought I wasn't supposed to have. Grace for my past self and the girl who didn't know any better. Grace for my future self, who will keep evolving.

Once I give myself grace and accept all the versions of myself, I find that grace is not something we should only give when we think we've messed up; it's a state of being. It's a state of full self-love and acceptance, where the things we used to reject in ourselves are now looked at with appreciation, and even a sense of humor.

Grace is my inner "knowing" that I am an extension of an endless flow of love and approval, and that I am always exactly where I am supposed to be.

Look at the darkest parts of yourself and thank them for teaching you to how to love.

—MAREN SWENSON, Glow Coach & Founder of Wild Serenity, Utah (USA)

ACKNOWLEDGMENTS

I would like to begin by acknowledging that the land on which this work was created is the traditional and ancestral homeland of the Wisconsin First Nations, including the Menominee, Ho-Chunk, Ojibwe/Chippewa, Potawatomi, Oneida nations and all first people of this land who are not identified with the listed tribes. I would also like to acknowledge the indigenous peoples of my birth state of California, including the Kumeyaay (also known as Diegueño), La Jollan, Cuyamaca, Luiseño, Cupeño, Pauma, Cahuilla, Ohlone, Tongva, and Chumash tribes, and all first people of this land who are not identified with the listed tribes. I honor and respect the enduring connection these first nations have with these lands.

My deepest gratitude goes to my family. To Eddie: I am grateful for the chapter we shared, and above all, for the gift of our children. To my children, Tyler, Mateo, and Amaia: your joy and laughter are my daily inspiration and my reason to keep going.

To my mom: thank you for teaching me that change is always possible and for always having my back. Gratitude to my stepfather Arlie and my sister Faith: your unwavering belief in me has carried me through many challenges. Eternal love to my brother Craig, whose inspiration continues to guide me and who would have been overjoyed to see this book published. May he rest in peace until we meet again among the stars, and for all my ancestors whose perseverance allowed me to be here today.

Infinite gratitude to my dearly departed soul sister Lesa DeBergh, and my first spiritual teachers Tony and Linda Somlai, who all consistently pointed me back to the light within myself and reminded me that our journey on Earth is only a fraction of who we truly are.

I also extend special acknowledgment and heartfelt thanks to the women who courageously shared their stories and inspiration in this book. Your contributions keep the heart of this work flowing and growing.

I am deeply thankful to all my clients, friends, retreat participants, and business and soul partners, past, present, and future, who have entrusted me to be a part of their journeys.

Deep gratitude to the Onyx Publishing team, especially Hayley and Faye, for always cheering me on and making sure that this work does not live only in my head, but that it is shared with those who are ready to receive it.

Lastly, to you, dear Goddess: thank you for your commitment to growth, self-love, and building communities where everyone is valued. You are worthy. You are loved.

RESOURCES

Goddess Activation Hour Mini-Retreat
www.goddessoflightretreats.com/goddessgift

Printable Ho'oponopono Prayer
www.goddessoflightretreats.com/hp

Earth Grounding Five-Minute Meditation
www.goddessoflightretreats.com/meditation5

Future Self Journaling Prompts
www.goddessoflightretreats.com/prompts

Guided Visualization for Abundance
www.goddessoflightretreats.com/visualize

Abundance Wheel of Life Course
www.goddessoflightretreats.com/wheel

52 Goddess Celebrations Guide
www.goddessoflightretreats.com/celebrate

Connect with me at hello@goddessoflightretreats.com

All current offers and events can be found at
www.goddessoflightretreats.com

STUDY GUIDE / BOOK CLUB GUIDE

———

I highly recommend getting a group together, either in person or virtually, and reading *Messages from Your Future Self* chapter by chapter. Once you have finished reading each chapter, read and reflect on the corresponding questions in this section for an even more powerful experience.

A wonderful alternative is to read this book alone and use these questions as journaling prompts to help guide you deeper into your journey as you integrate the wisdom of this book into your life.

Feel free to share your insights and self-discoveries on the Goddess of Light Retreats social media platforms too!

Chapter 1

- Is there anything (tasks, expectations, relationships, or judgments) you need to release before you can fully step into life as your future self?
- What does self-compassion mean to you?
- Where could you apply the concept of Wabi Sabi in your life right now?

Chapter 2

- Have you ever done energy work/healing? What was the experience like for you?
- Reflect on this quote by Rumi: "The wound is the place where the light enters." What have you overcome that felt painful in the moment but turned into an opportunity for healing or helping?
- What recommendations from Chapter 2 do you believe would be beneficial for you to implement today?

Chapter 3

- What are some key differences between mind-based fear and intuitive fear?
- What is an example of a time you trusted your intuition and learned that you made the right choice, despite there being no logical reason at the time for why you made the decision you did?
- Could you describe a time when you had a mind-based fear that you courageously overcame? How did you move through the feelings of discomfort?

Chapter 4

- Why are self-promises so important?
- Have you ever broken a promise to yourself? What was the outcome of the broken promise, and how did you feel afterward?
- What is a self-promise you are going to make now to your future self?

Chapter 5

- Can you recall a time when your actions, words, decisions, or appearance were dictated by a wish to please someone else, and this felt incongruent with who you really are? What did you learn from that experience?
- What is an example of something you have accomplished that you thought was nearly impossible at first? What did it take for you to reach that goal?
- Describe your future self. Where does she live or work? What are her self-beliefs and thoughts? What is it about her that makes you excited to step into her shoes?

Chapter 6

- Have you ever used visualization? If so, what did you visualize, and what was the result?
- Do you know any additional examples of people (famous or otherwise) who use visualization to help them achieve their goals?
- If visualization is typically associated with the third eye chakra, why do you think this chapter also encouraged you to open the root and sacral chakras while practicing visualization?

Chapter 7

- Have you ever been to a retreat before? What was your experience like?
- Have you ever traveled somewhere that completely opened your eyes to something new or touched your heart in a way that will eternally be with you?
- Describe your ideal retreat. Who is there? What type of activities do you engage in? What is the environment like? What do you experience? Use the power of your imagination to create this personalized retreat in your mind's eye.

Chapter 8

- Have you ever explored your genius zone? If yes, describe in as much detail as possible some aspects of your zone of genius. If not, what are some things that seem to come naturally to you that you truly enjoy doing?
- Where in your life could the 1% Rule or Kaizen principle help you to create sustainable change?
- What, if anything, needs to shift in your current daily routine so that you can move closer to a state of overflow and abundance?

Chapter 9

- Are you someone who is likely to create a plan and not deviate from it? Or do you go with what feels right at that moment? Perhaps you are somewhere in between? In this moment, do you need to allow for more flexibility and adaptation in your approach to life, or more structure?

- Is there anything in your environment that needs to be changed or altered to help you take inspired action with more ease and joy?

- Share some different ways in which you will celebrate after you have taken inspired action.

Chapter 10

- Which Goddess in this book did you resonate with the most?

- Which Goddess do you want to embody or learn from to a greater degree?

- What was your biggest takeaway from *Messages from Your Future Self*?

- What inspired action will you be taking now?

www.ingramcontent.com/pod-product-compliance
Lightning Source LLC
Chambersburg PA
CBHW021143090426
42740CB00008B/915